Introduction

The motifs in this book are squares or hexagons that can be tiled together to make fabric. Squares are fantastic because they make a nice straight edge around the perimeter. Hexagons do not make a straight edge around the perimeter; they make an uneven outer edge, which can be quite beautiful. Sometimes, though, the project could be improved by "filling in" the outer edge of a hexagon project or adding some diagonals to a square project. In this book you will learn how to make half motifs. That is, you will learn to take a square motif, keep the integrity of the design, but only make part of it. Also, you will learn to make half hexagons, which will neatly fill in edges and give you more flexibility when building a project.

READING STITCH DIAGRAMS

All the motifs and projects in this book have both written word instructions and diagrammed symbol instructions. The visual diagram is another way of communicating the same information as the written text. The stitch diagram offers another way to learn to make the project. You can refer to both sets of instructions or use the one that is easier for you.

Each symbol in a stitch diagram represents one stitch. When following a stitch diagram in rounds, begin in the center and read the diagram outward in a counterclockwise direction. If you are left-handed, you will read the diagram in a clockwise direction. The full motifs are not turned; that is, all rounds are worked on the right side. Half motifs are sometimes turned at the end of the row and sometimes not, so you'll have to pay attention. Also, full motifs are worked in rounds, whereas half motifs are worked in rows that are either turned or fastened off at the end. When the next row or round begins, the diagram will indicate the change with a change in color as well as the stitches needed to join and begin the new row or round.

THE WHY OF HALF MOTIFS

Half motifs either fill in space or add shape. For example, in the Scarf, the half motifs that hug the full ones create a straight edge along the long side. When crocheters are ready to make the jump from blankets and scarves to garments, motif sweaters are a great choice. Using squares, a straight neckline can be turned into a V-neckline by replacing a few full motifs with triangular "half" squares.

I use the term half motif somewhat loosely. A square has four corners, so you would expect half of a square to have two corners. Mathematically, if a square begins with a round of eight single crochets, you might expect that the half motif would begin with four. Throw these ideas out the window. Mostly, we need to construct the motif so that it will fit where it needs to go. There will be a few extra stitches in the instructions added into the pattern so that the half motif can anchor or connect logically to its neighbor.

The same is true with hexagons. Hexagons have six sides and six corners. To make half of a hexagon, you might logically assume that it would have three sides and three corners. To fill the edge space of a group of hexagons, one of the sides will have deep spaces (like in the Scarf pattern). To fill that space, connecting all the corners and leaving no gaps, the half motif will need to have three sides and four corners.

If you don't want to think about HOW to make a full motif into a half, don't worry. Every motif in this book has an accompanying half version. Some of the squares have half motifs that are rectangles and some that are triangles. If you DO want to make any motif into a half motif, look at the stitch diagram for the full version. Cover the half you don't want with a piece of paper. The half that is still exposed is what you will try to re-create. You will need to add stitches on either end to make the corners, use your pencil to draw in the turning chains that would be appropriate when turning to the next row and use rows instead of rounds. Give it a try! ■

Scarf Hexagon

SKILL LEVEL

EASY

FINISHED MEASUREMENTS
Motif: 4¾ inches x 4¾ inches (side to side)

Half Motif: 5½ inches wide x 2¾ inches tall

MATERIALS
- Plymouth Encore Worsted medium (worsted) weight acrylic/wool yarn (3½ oz/200 yds/100g per ball):
    4 yds #137 California pink (A)
    2 yds #458 purple orchid (B)
    1 yd #1308 beach berry (C)
- Size I/9/5.5mm crochet hook or size needed to obtain gauge
- Tapestry needle

GAUGE
Motif = 4¾ inches (blocked)

Take time to check gauge.

PATTERN NOTES
Weave in ends as work progresses.

Join with slip stitch as indicated unless otherwise stated.

Chain-4 at beginning of round counts as a treble crochet unless otherwise stated.

SPECIAL STITCHES
Beginning bobble (beg bobble): Ch 1 loosely, *yo and draw up lp 4 times in st indicated, yo and draw through all lps on hook.

Bobble (bobble): *Yo and draw up lp 4 times in st indicated, yo and draw through all lps on hook.

MOTIF
Rnd 1 (RS): With B, ch 4, **join** *(see Pattern Notes)* in first ch to form ring, ch 1, 6 sc in ring, join in first sc. *(6 sc)*

Rnd 2: Beg bobble *(see Special Stitches)* in same st as joining, ch 3, [**bobble** *(see Special Stitches)* in next st, ch 3] 5 times, join in top of beg bobble. Fasten off. *(6 bobbles, 6 ch-3 sps)*

Rnd 3: Join C with sc in top of any bobble, 3 sc in next ch-3 sp, [sc in top of next bobble, 3 sc in next ch-3 sp] 5 times, join in first sc. Fasten off. *(24 sc)*

Rnd 4: Join A in sc over any bobble, **ch 4** *(see Pattern Notes)*, 4 tr in same st, *ch 3, sk next 3 sts **, 5 tr in next st, rep from * around, ending last rep at **, join in 4th ch of beg ch-4. *(30 tr, 6 ch-3 sps)*

Rnd 5: Ch 1, sc in same ch as beg ch-1, sc in next st, *(sc, ch 5, sc) in next st, sc in each of next 2 sts, 3 sc in next ch-3 sp**, sc in each of next 2 sts, rep from * around, ending last rep at **, join in first sc. Fasten off. *(54 sc, 6 ch-5 sps)*

HALF MOTIF

Row 1 (RS): With A, ch 4, **join** *(see Pattern Notes)* in first ch to form ring, ch 1, 4 sc in ring, turn. *(4 sc)*

Row 2: Beg bobble *(see Special Stitches)* in first st, [ch 3, **bobble** *(see Special Stitches)* in next st] 3 times. Fasten off. *(4 bobbles, 3 ch-3 sps)*

Row 3: With WS facing, join C with sc in first bobble, [3 sc in next ch-3 sp, sc in next bobble] 3 times. Fasten off. *(13 sc)*

Row 4: With RS facing, join B in first st, ch 4 *(see Pattern Notes)*, 2 tr in same st, [ch 3, sk next 3 sc, 5 tr in next sc] twice, ch 3, sk next 3 sc, 3 tr in last sc, turn. *(16 tr, 3 ch-3 sps)*

Row 5: Ch 1, (sc, ch 5, sc) in first st, [sc in each of next 2 tr, 3 sc in next ch-3 sp, sc in each of next 2 tr, (sc, ch 5, sc) in next tr] 3 times. Fasten off. *(4 ch-5 sps, 29 sc)* ∎

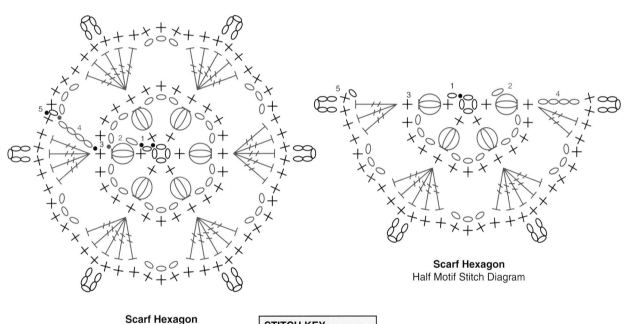

Scarf Hexagon
Motif Stitch Diagram

Scarf Hexagon
Half Motif Stitch Diagram

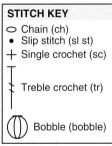

STITCH KEY
◯ Chain (ch)
• Slip stitch (sl st)
+ Single crochet (sc)
⌠ Treble crochet (tr)
⬭ Bobble (bobble)

Cowl Hexagon

SKILL LEVEL

EASY

FINISHED MEASUREMENTS

Motif: 4½ inches across

Half Motif: 4¼ inches wide x 2½ inches tall

MATERIALS
- Plymouth Encore Worsted medium (worsted) weight acrylic/wool yarn (3½ oz/200 yds/100g per ball):
  4 yds #453 rust roadster (A)
  2 yds #355 garnet mix (B)
- Size J/10/6mm crochet hook or size needed to obtain gauge
- Tapestry needle

GAUGE
Motif = 4½ inches across (blocked)

Take time to check gauge.

PATTERN NOTES
Weave in ends as work progresses.

Join with slip stitch as indicated unless otherwise stated.

Chain-3 at beginning of round counts as a double crochet unless otherwise stated.

Chain-6 at beginning of row counts as a double crochet and chain-3 space unless otherwise stated.

SPECIAL STITCH
Cluster (cl): Holding back last lp of each st on hook, 3 dc as indicated in instructions, yo, pull through 4 loops on hook.

MOTIF
Rnd 1 (RS): With B, ch 5, **join** (*see Pattern Notes*) in first ch to form ring, **ch 3** (*see Pattern Notes*), 11 dc in ring, join in 3rd ch of beg ch-3. Fasten off. (*12 dc*)

Rnd 2: Working in **back lps** (*see Stitch Guide*), join A with sc in any st, sc in same st, 2 sc in each rem st around, join in first sc. (*24 sc*)

Rnd 3: Ch 1, sc in same st as beg ch-1, ch 5, sk next 3 sts, [sc in next st, ch 5, sk next 3 sts] 5 times, join in first sc. *(6 sc, 6 ch-5 sps)*

Rnd 4: Ch 1, sc in same sc as beg ch-1, *ch 2, (**cl**—*see Special Stitch*, ch 3, cl) in next ch-5 sp, ch 2**, sc in next st, rep from * around, ending last rep at **, join in first sc. Fasten off. *(12 cls, 6 sc, 12 ch-2 sps, 6 ch-3 sps)*

HALF MOTIF
Row 1 (WS): With B, ch 5, **join** *(see Pattern Notes)* in first ch to form ring, ch 3, 6 dc in ring. Fasten off. *(7 dc)*

Row 2 (RS): With RS facing and working in **back lps** *(see Stitch Guide)*, join A with sc in first st, 2 sc in each rem st across, turn. *(13 sc)*

Row 3: Ch 1, sc in first st, ch 3, sk next st, sc in next st, ch 5, sk next 3 sts, sc in next st, ch 5, sk next 3 sts, sc in next st, ch 3, sk next st, sc in last st, turn. *(5 sc, 2 ch-5 sps, 2 ch-3 sps)*

Row 4: Ch 6 *(see Pattern Notes)*, **cl** *(see Special Stitch)* in next ch-3 sp, ch 2, [sc in next sc, ch 2, (cl, ch 3, cl) in next ch-5 sp, ch 2] twice, sc in next sc, ch 2, cl in next ch-3 sp, ch 3, dc in last sc. Fasten off. *(6 cls, 4 ch-3 sps, 6 ch-2 sps, 3 sc, 2 dc)* ∎

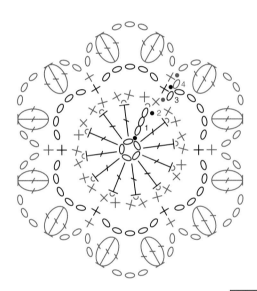

Cowl Hexagon
Motif Stitch Diagram

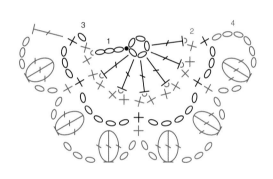

Cowl Hexagon
Half Motif Stitch Diagram

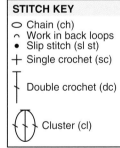

STITCH KEY
⬭ Chain (ch)
⌢ Work in back loops
● Slip stitch (sl st)
+ Single crochet (sc)
┃ Double crochet (dc)
⬭ Cluster (cl)

Hat Hexagon

SKILL LEVEL

INTERMEDIATE

FINISHED MEASUREMENTS

Motif: 5½ inches across

Half Motif: 5½ inches wide x 2½ inches tall

MATERIALS

- Plymouth Encore Worsted medium (worsted) weight acrylic/wool yarn (3½ oz/200 yds/100g per ball): 5 yds #1385 bright fuchsia
- Size I/9/5.5mm crochet hook or size needed to obtain gauge
- Tapestry needle

GAUGE

Motif = 5½ inches (blocked)

Take time to check gauge.

PATTERN NOTES

Join with slip stitch as indicated unless otherwise stated.

Chain-3 at beginning of round or row counts as a double crochet unless otherwise stated.

MOTIF

Rnd 1 (RS): Ch 4, **join** (*see Pattern Notes*) in first ch to form ring, **ch 3** (*see Pattern Notes*), 11 dc in ring, join in 3rd ch of beg ch-3. (*12 dc*)

Rnd 2: Ch 1, (sc, ch 9, sc) in same ch as beg ch-1, (sc, ch 5, sc) in next st, [(sc, ch 9, sc) in next st, (sc, ch 5, sc) in next st] 5 times, join in first sc. (*6 ch-9 sps, 6 ch-5 sps*)

Rnd 3: Sl st in each of first 4 chs of next ch-9 sp, ch 1, 3 sc in same sp, *ch 2, sc in next ch-5 sp, ch 2, 3 sc in next ch-9 sp, rep from * 4 times, ch 2, sc in next ch-5 sp, ch 2, join in first sc. (*24 sc, 12 ch-2 sps*)

Rnd 4: Ch 1, sc in same st as beg ch-1, *(sc, ch 5, sc) in next st, sc in next st, 2 sc in next ch-2 sp, sc in next st, 2 sc in next ch-2 sp**, sc in next st, rep from * around, ending last rep at **, join in first sc. Fasten off. (*54 sc, 6 ch-5 sps*)

HALF MOTIF

Row 1 (WS): Ch 3, **join** *(see Pattern Notes)* in first ch to form ring, **ch 3** *(see Pattern Notes)*, 6 dc in ring, do not join, turn. *(7 dc)*

Row 2 (RS): Ch 9, sc in first st, *(sc, ch 5, sc) in next st, (sc, ch 9, sc) in next st, rep from * once, (sc, ch 5, sc) in next st, (sc, ch 9, sl st) in last st, turn. *(4 ch-9 sps, 3 ch-5 sps, 12 sc)*

Row 3: Sl st in each of first 4 chs of next ch-9 sp, 2 sc in same sp, *ch 2, sc in next ch-5 sp, ch 2, 3 sc in next ch-9 sp, rep from * once, ch 2, sc in next ch-5 sp, ch 2, 2 sc in next ch-9 sp, turn. *(13 sc, 6 ch-2 sps)*

Row 4: Ch 1, sc in first st, ch 5, *sc in next st, 2 sc in next ch-2 sp, sc in next st, 2 sc in next ch-2 sp, sc in next st, (sc, ch 5, sc) in next st, rep from * once, sc in next st, 2 sc in next ch-2 sp, sc in next st, 2 sc in next ch-2 sp, sc in next st, ch 5, sc in last st. Fasten off. *(27 sc, 4 ch-5 sps)* ■

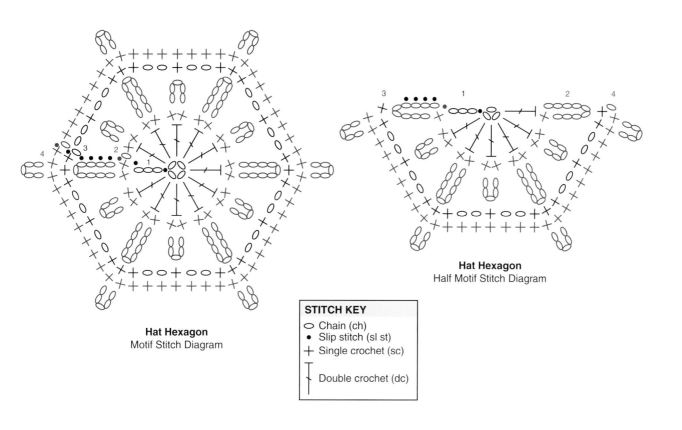

Hat Hexagon
Motif Stitch Diagram

Hat Hexagon
Half Motif Stitch Diagram

STITCH KEY
⟠ Chain (ch)
● Slip stitch (sl st)
+ Single crochet (sc)

Ŧ Double crochet (dc)

Cluster Granny Square

SKILL LEVEL

■■□□

EASY

FINISHED MEASUREMENTS

Motif: 4½ inches x 4½ inches

Half Motif: 5 inches wide x 2¾ inches tall

MATERIALS

- Plymouth Encore Worsted medium (worsted) weight acrylic/wool yarn (3½ oz/200 yds/100g per ball):
  4 yds #1308 beach berry (A)
  3 yds #473 aquarius (B)
- Size I/9/5.5mm crochet hook or size needed to obtain gauge
- Tapestry needle

GAUGE

Motif = 4½ inches x 4½ inches (blocked)

Take time to check gauge.

PATTERN NOTES

Weave in ends as work progresses.

Join with slip stitch as indicated unless otherwise stated.

Chain-3 at beginning of round counts as a double crochet unless otherwise stated.

SPECIAL STITCHES

Beginning cluster (beg cl): Ch 3, holding back last lp of each st on hook, 2 dc in same sp or st as beg ch-3, yo, draw through 3 lps on hook.

Cluster (cl): Holding back last lp of each st on hook, 3 dc in sp or st indicated, yo, draw through 4 lps on hook.

MOTIF

Rnd 1 (RS): With B, ch 4, **join** *(see Pattern Notes)* in first ch to form ring, **beg cl** *(see Special Stitches)* in ring, ch 4, [cl *(see Special Stitches)* in ring, ch 4] 3 times, join in top of beg cl. *(4 cls)*

Rnd 2: Beg cl in same st as joining, ch 2, *(cl, ch 3, cl) in next ch-4 sp, ch 2, cl in next cl, ch 2, rep from * twice, (cl, ch 3, cl) in next ch-4 sp, ch 2, join in top of beg cl. Fasten off. *(12 cls, 4 ch-3 sps, 8 ch-2 sps)*

Rnd 3: Join A in any ch-3 sp, (beg cl, ch 5, cl) in same sp, ch 3, sk next cl and ch-2 sp, cl in next cl, ch 3, *(cl, ch 5, cl) in next ch-3 sp, ch 3, sk next ch-2 sp, cl in next cl, ch 3, rep from * twice, join in top of beg cl. *(12 cls, 8 ch-3 sps, 4 ch-5 sps)*

Rnd 4: Ch 1, working in **back lps** *(see Stitch Guide)*, sc in same cl as beg ch-1, *sc in each of next 2 chs, 3 sc in next ch *(corner made)*, sc in each of next 2 chs, sc in next cl, sc in each of next 3 chs, sc in next cl, sc in each of next 3 chs**, sc in next cl, rep from * 3 times, ending last rep at **, join in first sc. Fasten off. *(60 sc)*

HALF MOTIF

Row 1 (WS): With B, ch 4, **join** *(see Pattern Notes)* in first ch to form ring, **beg cl** *(see Special Stitches)* in ring, [ch 4, **cl** *(see Special Stitches)* in ring] twice, turn. *(3 cls, 2 ch-4 sps)*

Row 2: Beg cl in first cl, ch 2, (cl, ch 3, cl) in next ch-4 sp, ch 2, cl in next cl, ch 2, (cl, ch 3, cl) in next ch-4 sp, ch 2, cl in last cl. Fasten off. *(7 cls, 2 ch-3 sps, 4 ch-2 sps)*

Row 3: With WS facing, join A in first st, beg cl in same st, ch 3, (cl, ch 5, cl) in next ch-3 sp, ch 3, sk next cl, cl in next cl, ch 3, sk next cl, (cl, ch 5, cl) in next ch-3 corner sp, ch 3, sk next cl, cl in last cl, turn. *(7 cls, 2 ch-5 sps, 4 ch-3 sps)*

Row 4: Ch 1, working in **back lps** *(see Stitch Guide)*, sc in of each of first 7 sts and chs, 3 sc in next ch, sc in each of next 13 sts and chs, 3 sc in next ch, sc in each of next 7 sts. Fasten off. *(33 sc)* ∎

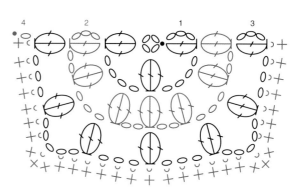

Cluster Square
Half Motif Stitch Diagram

Cluster Square
Motif Stitch Diagram

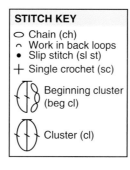

STITCH KEY

◯ Chain (ch)
⌒ Work in back loops
● Slip stitch (sl st)
+ Single crochet (sc)

Beginning cluster (beg cl)

Cluster (cl)

Archetypal Square

SKILL LEVEL

EASY

FINISHED MEASUREMENTS
Motif: 5 inches x 5 inches

Half Motif: 5 inches wide x 3 inches tall

MATERIALS
- Plymouth Encore Worsted medium (worsted) weight acrylic/wool yarn (3½ oz/200 yds/100g per ball):
  4 yds each #137 California pink (A) and #458 purple orchid (B)
  2 yds #449 pink (C)
- Size I/9/5.5mm crochet hook or size needed to obtain gauge
- Tapestry needle

GAUGE
Motif = 5 inches x 5 inches (blocked)

Take time to check gauge.

PATTERN NOTES
Weave in ends as work progresses.

Join with slip stitch as indicated unless otherwise stated.

Chain-3 at beginning of round or row counts as a double crochet unless otherwise stated.

Chain-5 at beginning of round or row counts as a double crochet and chain-2 space unless otherwise stated.

MOTIF
Rnd 1 (RS): With C, ch 4, **join** (*see Pattern Notes*) in first ch to form ring, ch 1, 8 sc in ring, join in first sc. (*8 sc*)

Rnd 2: Ch 3 (*see Pattern Notes*), 2 dc in same st, *ch 3, sk next st, 3 dc in next st, rep from * twice, ch 3, sk next st, join in 3rd ch of beg ch-3. Fasten off. (*12 dc, 4 ch-3 sps*)

Rnd 3: Join A with sc in same ch as joining, *ch 2, sk next st, sc in next st, (sc, ch 3, sc) in next ch-3 sp**, sc in next st, rep from * around, ending last rep at **, join in first sc. (*4 ch-3 sps, 4 ch-2 sps, 16 sc*)

Rnd 4: Ch 5 (*see Pattern Notes*), *dc in each of next 2 sts, ch 5**, dc in each of next 2 sc, ch 2, rep from * around, ending last rep at **, dc in next st, join in 3rd ch of beg ch-5. Fasten off. (*16 dc, 4 ch-2 sps, 4 ch-5 sps*)

Rnd 5: Join B with dc in same ch as joining, ch 2, *dc in each of next 2 sts, ch 7, dc in each of next 2 sts, ch 2, rep from * twice, dc in each of next 2 sts, ch 7, dc in next dc, join in first dc. (*16 dc, 4 ch-2 sps, 4 ch-7 sps*)

Rnd 6: Ch 1, sc in same st as beg ch-1, *3 sc in next ch-2 sp, sc in each of next 2 dc, (3 sc, hdc, dc, hdc, 3 sc) in next ch-7 sp**, sc in each of next 2 dc, rep from * around, ending last rep at **, sc in next dc, join in first sc. Fasten off. *(4 dc, 8 hdc, 52 sc)*

HALF MOTIF
Row 1 (WS): With C, ch 4, **join** *(see Pattern Notes)* in first ch to form ring, ch 1, 5 sc in ring, turn. *(5 sc)*

Row 2 (RS): Ch 3 *(see Pattern Notes)*, 2 dc in first sc, ch 3, sk next sc, 3 dc in next sc, ch 3, sk next sc, 3 dc in last sc. Fasten off. *(9 dc, 2 ch-3 sps)*

Row 3: With WS facing, join A with sc in first st, ch 2, sk next st, sc in next st, (sc, ch 3, sc) in next ch-3 sp, sc in next st, ch 2, sk next st, sc in next st, (sc, ch 3, sc) in next ch-3 sp, sc in next st, ch 2, sk next st, sc in last st, turn. *(10 sc, 5 ch-3 sps)*

Row 4: Ch 5 *(see Pattern Notes)*, dc in each of next 2 sts, ch 5, dc in each of next 2 sts, ch 2 dc in each of next 2 sts, ch 5, dc in each of next 2 sts, ch 2, dc in last st. Fasten off. *(10 dc, 3 ch-3 sps, 2 ch-5 sps)*

Row 5: With WS facing, join B with dc in first st, ch 2, dc in each of next 2 sts, ch 7, dc in each of next 2 sts, ch 2, dc in each of next 2 sts, ch 7, dc in each of next 2 sts, ch 2, dc in last st, turn. *(10 dc, 3 ch-2 sps, 2 ch-7 sps)*

Row 6: Ch 1, sc in first st, *3 sc in next ch-2 sp, sc in each of next 2 sts, (3 sc, hdc, dc, hdc, 3 sc) in next ch-7 sp, sc in each of next 2 sts, rep from * once, 3 sc in next ch-2 sp, sc in last st. Fasten off. *(2 dc, 4 hdc, 31 sc)* ∎

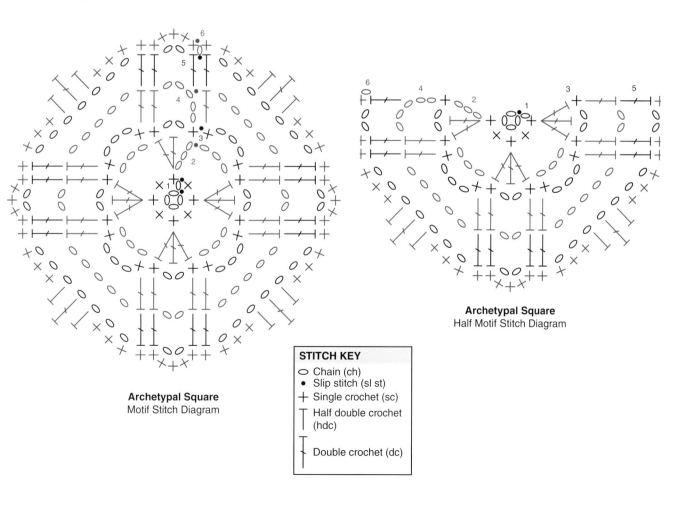

Archetypal Square
Motif Stitch Diagram

Archetypal Square
Half Motif Stitch Diagram

STITCH KEY
○ Chain (ch)
• Slip stitch (sl st)
+ Single crochet (sc)
⊤ Half double crochet (hdc)
Double crochet (dc)

Gray Square

SKILL LEVEL

EASY

FINISHED MEASUREMENTS

Motif: 6 inches x 6 inches

Half Motif: 7½ inches x 4 inches

MATERIALS

- Plymouth Encore Worsted medium (worsted) weight acrylic/wool yarn (3½ oz/200 yds/100g per ball):
  4 yds #256 ecru (A)
  2 yds #149 periwinkle heather (B)
- Size I/9/5.5mm crochet hook or size needed to obtain gauge
- Tapestry needle

GAUGE

Motif = 6 inches x 6 inches (blocked)

Take time to check gauge.

PATTERN NOTES

Weave in ends as work progresses.

Join with slip stitch as indicated unless otherwise stated.

Chain-6 at beginning of round or row counts as a treble crochet and chain-2 space unless otherwise stated.

Chain-5 at beginning of round counts as a double crochet and chain-2 space unless otherwise stated.

Chain-4 at beginning of round counts as a treble crochet unless otherwise stated.

SPECIAL STITCHES

Beginning V-stitch (beg V-st): Ch 5 (*see Pattern Notes*), dc in same st as beg ch-5.

V-stitch (V-st): (Dc, ch 2, dc) in same st or sp.

Picot: Ch 3, hdc in 3rd ch from hook.

MOTIF

Rnd 1 (RS): With B, ch 4, **join** (*see Pattern Notes*) in first ch to form ring, **ch 6** (*see Pattern Notes*), [tr in ring, ch 2] 7 times, join in 4th ch of beg ch-6. (*8 tr, 8 ch-2 sps*)

Rnd 2: Beg V-st (*see Special Stitches*) in same ch as joining, ch 2, sk next ch-2 sp, *V-st (*see Special Stitches*) in next st, ch 2, sk next ch-2 sp, rep from * around, join in 3rd ch of beg ch-5. (*8 V-sts, 8 ch-2 sps*)

Rnd 3: Ch 6, dc in same ch as beg ch-6, V-st in each of next 3 sts, *(dc, ch 3, dc) in next st (*corner made*), V-st in each of next 3 sts, rep from * twice, join in 3rd ch of beg ch-6. Fasten off. (*12 V-sts, 8 dc, 4 ch-3 sps*)

Rnd 4: Join A in ch-3 sp of any corner, **ch 4** (*see Pattern Notes*), (3 tr, **picot**—*see Special Stitches*, 4 tr) in same ch-3 sp as beg ch-4, *ch 4, **tr dec** (*see Stitch Guide*) in next 3 ch-2 sps, ch 4**, (4 tr, picot, 4 tr) in next ch-3 corner sp, rep from * 3 times, ending last rep at **, join in 4th ch of beg ch-4. Fasten off. (*32 tr, 4 picots, 8 ch-4 sps*)

HALF MOTIF
Row 1 (WS): With B, ch 4, **join** (*see Pattern Notes*) in first ch to form ring, **ch 6** (*see Pattern Notes*), [tr in ring, ch 2] 3 times, tr in ring, turn. (*5 tr, 4 ch-2 sps*)

Row 2 (RS): **Beg V-st** (*see Special Stitches*) in first st, ch 2, sk next ch-2 sp, [**V-st** (*see Special Stitches*) in next st, ch 2, sk next ch-2 sp] 3 times, dc in last st, turn. (*4 V-sts, 1 dc, 4 ch-2 sps*)

Row 3: Ch 6, dc in first st, V-st in each of next 3 sts, (dc, ch 3, dc) in next dc, V-st in each of next 3 sts, (dc, ch 3, dc) in last dc. Fasten off. (*6 V-sts, 6 dc, 3 ch-3 sps*)

Row 4: With RS facing, join A with tr in first ch-3 sp, **picot** (*see Special Stitches*), 4 tr in same sp, ch 4, **tr dec** (*see Stitch Guide*) in next 3 ch-2 sps, ch 4, (4 tr, picot, 4 tr) in next ch-3 sp, ch 4, tr dec in next 3 ch-2 sps, ch 4, (4 tr, picot, tr in last ch sp. Fasten off. (*18 tr, 3 picots, 4 ch-4 sps*) ■

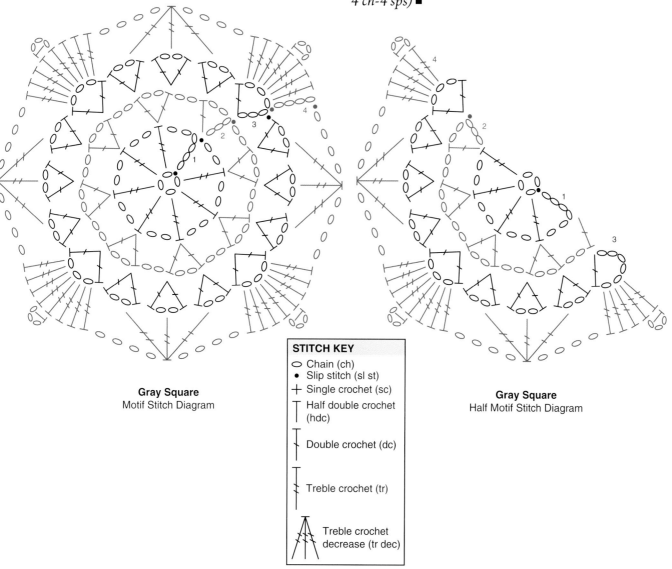

Gray Square
Motif Stitch Diagram

Gray Square
Half Motif Stitch Diagram

STITCH KEY
⬭ Chain (ch)
• Slip stitch (sl st)
+ Single crochet (sc)
T Half double crochet (hdc)
‡ Double crochet (dc)
‡ Treble crochet (tr)
Ж Treble crochet decrease (tr dec)

Flower Hexagon

SKILL LEVEL

EASY

FINISHED MEASUREMENTS
Motif: 4½ inches x 4½ inches (side to side)

Half Motif: 5 inches wide x 4½ inches tall

MATERIALS
- Plymouth Encore Worsted medium (worsted) weight acrylic/wool yarn (3½ oz/200 yds/100g per ball):
    4 yds #452 purple prelude (A)
    2 yds #1308 beach berry (B)
- Size I/9/5.5mm crochet hook or size needed to obtain gauge
- Tapestry needle

GAUGE
Motif = 4½ inches x 4½ inches (blocked)

Take time to check gauge.

PATTERN NOTES
Weave in ends as work progresses.

Join with slip stitch as indicated unless otherwise stated.

Chain-4 at beginning of round or row counts as a treble crochet unless otherwise stated.

MOTIF
Rnd 1 (RS): With A, ch 4, **join** (see Pattern Notes) in first ch to form ring, ch 1, 12 sc in ring, join in first sc. (12 sc)

Rnd 2: Ch 1, working in **back lps** (see Stitch Guide), sc in same st as beg ch-1, ch 5, sk next sc, [sc in next sc, ch 5, sk next sc] 5 times, join in first sc. (6 sc, 6 ch-5 sps)

Rnd 3: Sl st in each of next 2 chs of next ch-5 sp, **ch 4** (see Pattern Notes), 4 tr in same ch-5 sp, ch 2, *5 tr in next ch-5 sp, ch 2, rep from * 4 times; join in 4th ch of beg ch-4. (30 tr, 6 ch-2 sps)

Rnd 4: Ch 1, sc in same st as beg ch-1, sc in next tr, *(sc, ch 5, sc) in next tr, sc in each of next 2 tr, 2 sc in next ch-2 sp**, sc in each of next 2 tr, rep from * around, ending last rep at **, join in first sc. Fasten off. (48 sc)

FLOWER
Join B in any unused **front lp** (see Stitch Guide) on rnd 1, ch 5, [sl st in next st, ch 5] 11 times, join in joining sl st. Fasten off. (12 ch-5 sps)

HALF MOTIF
Row 1 (RS): With A, ch 4, **join** (see Pattern Notes) in first ch to form ring, ch 1, 9 sc in ring, turn. (9 sc)

Row 2: Ch 1, working in **front lps** (see Stitch Guide), sc in first st, *ch 5, sk next st, sc in next st, rep from * across, turn. (5 sc, 4 ch-5 sps)

Row 3: Ch 1, sl st in each of next 2 chs of next ch-5 sp, **ch 4** *(see Pattern Notes)*, 2 tr in same sp, ch 2, [5 tr in next ch-5 sp, ch 2] twice, 3 tr in last ch-5 sp, turn. *(16 tr, 3 ch-2 sps)*

Row 4: Ch 1, (sc, ch 5, sc) in first st, sc in each of next 2 sts, *2 sc in next ch-2 sp, sc in each of next 2 sts, (sc, ch 5, sc) in next st, sc in each of next 2 sts, rep from * once, 2 sc in next ch-2 sp, sc in each of next 2 sts, (sc, ch 5, sc) in last st. Fasten off. *(26 sc, 4 ch-5 sps)*

FLOWER
With RS facing, join B in first unused lp on row 1, *ch 5, sl st in next unused lp, rep from * across. Fasten off. *(8 ch-5 sps)* ■

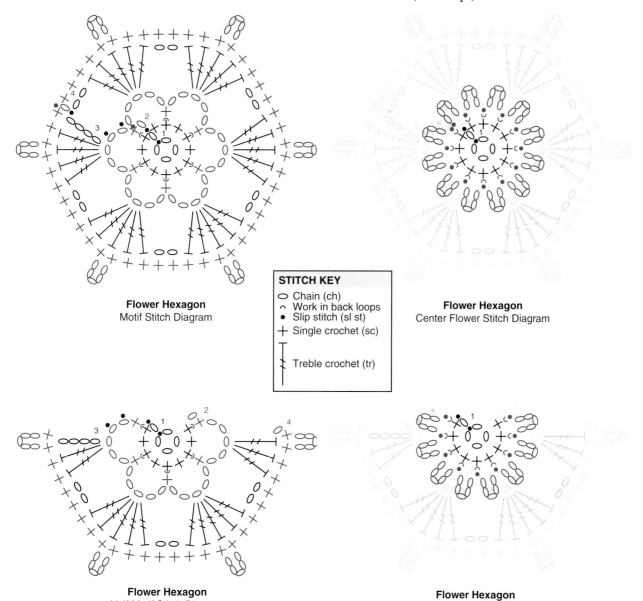

Flower Hexagon
Motif Stitch Diagram

STITCH KEY
⬭ Chain (ch)
⌒ Work in back loops
● Slip stitch (sl st)
+ Single crochet (sc)

⊺ Treble crochet (tr)

Flower Hexagon
Center Flower Stitch Diagram

Flower Hexagon
Half Motif Stitch Diagram

Flower Hexagon
Center Flower Stitch Diagram for Half Motif

Petite Square

SKILL LEVEL

INTERMEDIATE

FINISHED MEASUREMENTS
Motif: 5 inches x 5 inches

Half Motif: 6 inches x 3 inches

MATERIALS
- Plymouth Encore Worsted medium (worsted) weight acrylic/wool yarn (3½ oz/200 yds/100g per ball):
  4 yds #958 regular mauve (A)
  3 yds #1415 fawn mix (B)
  2 yds #959 mauvetone (C)
- Size I/9/5.5mm crochet hook or size needed to obtain gauge
- Tapestry needle

GAUGE
Motif = 5 inches (blocked)

Take time to check gauge.

PATTERN NOTES
Weave in ends as work progresses.

Join with slip stitch as indicated unless otherwise stated.

Chain-5 at beginning of round counts as a double crochet and chain-2 space unless otherwise stated.

Chain-4 at beginning of round counts as a double crochet and chain-1 space unless otherwise stated.

Chain-6 at beginning of row counts as a double crochet and chain-3 space unless otherwise stated.

SPECIAL STITCHES
Cluster (cl): Holding back last lp of each st on hook, 3 dc in indicated st, yo, draw through 4 lps on hook.

Beginning shell (Beg shell): Ch 4 *(see Pattern Notes)*, (dc, ch 1, dc) in indicated st.

Shell: ([Dc, ch 1] twice, dc) in indicated st.

Beginning cluster (beg cl): Ch 3, holding back last lp of each st on hook, 2 dc in same st as beg ch-3, yo, draw through all 3 lps on hook.

MOTIF
Rnd 1 (RS): With A, ch 4, **join** *(see Pattern Notes)* in first ch to form ring, ch 1, 8 sc in ring, join in first sc. *(8 sc)*

Rnd 2: Ch 5 *(see Pattern Notes)*, [**cl** *(see Special Stitches)* in next st, ch 2, dc in next st, ch 2] 3 times, cl in next st, ch 2, join in 3rd ch of beg ch-5. *(4 cls, 4 dc, 8 ch-2 sps)*

Rnd 3: Beg shell in same st as joining, *ch 1, (cl, ch 3, cl) in next st *(corner made)*, ch 1, **shell** *(see Special Stitches)* in next st, rep from * twice, ch 1, (cl, ch 3, cl) in next st *(corner made)*, ch 1, join in 3rd ch of beg ch-4. Fasten off. *(8 cls, 4 shells)*

Rnd 4: Join C with sc in any ch-3 corner sp, 2 sc in same sp *(beg sc corner made)*, *sc in each of next 8 sts and sps, sc in next cl**, 3 sc in next ch-3 corner sp *(sc corner made)*, rep from * 3 times, ending last rep at **, join in first sc. Fasten off. *(48 sc)*

Rnd 5: Working in **back lps** *(see Stitch Guide)*, join B with dc in 2nd sc of any sc corner, 2 dc in same st, *dc in each st across to 2nd sc of next sc corner, 3 dc in 2nd sc, rep from * twice, dc in each st across to first dc, join in first dc. Fasten off. *(56 dc)*

Rnd 6: Join A in joining sl st, sl st in each st around, join in first sl st. Fasten off. *(56 sl sts)*

HALF MOTIF
Row 1 (WS): With A, ch 4, **join** *(see Pattern Notes)* in first ch to form ring, ch 1, 5 sc in ring, turn. *(5 sc)*

Row 2 (RS): Beg cl *(see Special Stitches)* in first st, ch 2, dc in next st, ch 2, **cl** *(see Special Stitches)* in next st, ch 2, dc in next st, ch 2, cl in last st, turn *(3 cls, 2 dc, 4 ch-2 sps)*

Row 3: Ch 6 *(see Pattern Notes)*, cl in same st as beg ch-6, ch 1, **shell** *(see Special Stitches)* in next st, ch 1, (cl, ch 3, cl) in next cl, ch 1, shell in next st, ch 1, (cl, ch 3, dc) in last st. Fasten off. *(6 cls, 2 shells, 3 ch-3 sps)*

Row 4: With RS facing, join C with sc in first ch-3 sp, sc in same sp, sc in each of next 9 sts and sps, 3 sc in next ch-3 sp, sc in each of next 9 sts and sps, 2 sc in last ch-3 sp. Fasten off. *(25 sc)*

Row 5: With RS facing and working in **back lps** *(see Stitch Guide)*, join B with dc in first st, dc in same st, dc in each of next 11 sts, 3 dc in next st, dc in each of next 11 sts, 2 dc in last st. Fasten off. *(29 dc)*

Row 6: With RS facing, join A in first st, sl st in each rem st across. Fasten off. *(29 sl sts)* ■

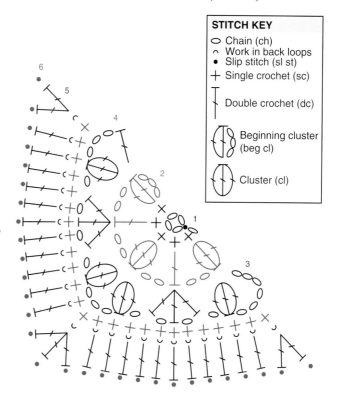

Petite Square
Motif Stitch Diagram

Petite Square
Half Motif Stitch Diagram

Loopy Square

SKILL LEVEL

EASY

FINISHED MEASUREMENTS
Motif: 7 inches x 7 inches

Half Motif: 7 inches x 3½ inches

MATERIALS
- Plymouth Encore Worsted medium (worsted) weight acrylic/wool yarn (3½ oz/200 yds/100g per ball):
  4 yds #137 California pink (A)
  3 yds #1606 purple bell (B)
- Size I/9/5.5mm crochet hook or size needed to obtain gauge
- Tapestry needle

GAUGE
Motif = 7 inches (blocked)

Take time to check gauge.

PATTERN NOTES
Weave in ends as work progresses.

Join with slip stitch as indicated unless otherwise stated.

Chain-3 at beginning of round or row counts as a double crochet unless otherwise stated.

MOTIF
Rnd 1 (RS): With A, ch 4, **join** (see Pattern Notes) in first ch to form ring, **ch 3** (see Pattern Notes), 11 dc in ring, join in 3rd ch of beg ch-3. (12 dc)

Rnd 2: Ch 1, sc in same st as beg ch-1, *ch 7, [sc in next st, ch 5] twice**, sc in next st, rep from * around, ending last rep at **, join in first sc. Fasten off. (4 ch-7 sps, 8 ch-5 sps)

Rnd 3: Join B with sc in any ch-7 sp, ch 5, sc in same sp (beg corner made), *ch 4, sk next ch-5 sp, dc in next st, ch 4, (sc, ch 5, sc) in next ch-7 sp (corner made), rep from * twice, ch 4, sk next ch-5 sp, dc in next sc, ch 4, sk next ch-5 sp, join in first sc. (4 dc, 8 sc, 8 ch-4 sps, 4 ch-5 corner sps)

Rnd 4: *(Sc, hdc, dc, tr, ch 3, tr, dc, hdc, sc) in next ch-5 corner sp, ch 2, 2 sc in next ch-4 sp, ch 2, (sc, ch 3, sc) in next st, ch 2, 2 sc in next ch-4 sp, ch 2, rep from * 3 times, join in first sc. Fasten off. (8 tr, 8 dc, 8 hdc, 32 sc)

HALF MOTIF

Row 1 (WS): With A, ch 4, **join** (*see Pattern Notes*) in first ch to form ring, **ch 3** (*see Pattern Notes*), 6 dc in ring, dc in ring, turn. (*7 dc*)

Row 2 (RS): Ch 7, sc in first st, [ch 5, sc in next st] twice, ch 7, sc in next st, [ch 5, sc in next st] twice, ch 7, sc in last st. Fasten off. (*3 ch-7 sps, 4 ch-5 sps*)

Row 3: With WS facing, join B with sc in first ch-7 sp, ch 5, sc in same sp, ch 4, sk next ch-5 sp, dc in next st, ch 4, sk next ch-5 sp, (sc, ch 5, sc) in next ch-7 sp, ch 4, sk next ch-5 sp, dc in next st, ch 4, sk next ch-5 sp, (sc, ch 5, sc) in last ch-7 sp, turn.

Row 4: Ch 1, sl st in each of first 2 chs of next ch-5 sp, ch 3, (tr, dc, hdc, sc) in same sp, ch 2, 2 sc in next ch-4 sp, ch 2, (sc, ch 5, sc) in next st, ch 2, 2 sc in next ch-4 sp, ch 2, (sc, hdc, dc, tr, ch 3, tr, dc, hdc, sc) in next ch-5 sp, ch 2, 2 sc in next ch-4 sp, ch 2, (sc, ch 3 sc) in next st, ch 2, 2 sc in next ch-4 sp, ch 2, (sc, hdc, dc, tr, ch 3) in next ch-5 sp, sl st in last 2 chs of same ch sp, Fasten off. ∎

Loopy Square
Motif Stitch Diagram

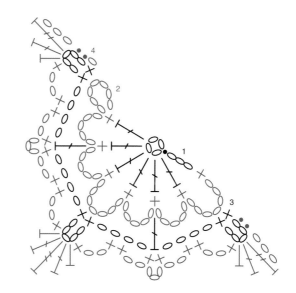

Loopy Square
Half Motif Stitch Diagram

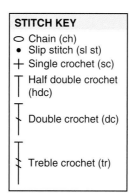

STITCH KEY
◯ Chain (ch)
● Slip stitch (sl st)
✛ Single crochet (sc)
⊤ Half double crochet (hdc)
† Double crochet (dc)
‡ Treble crochet (tr)

Star Square

SKILL LEVEL

INTERMEDIATE

FINISHED MEASUREMENTS

Motif: 4 inches x 4 inches

Half Motif: 6 inches x 3 inches

MATERIALS

- Plymouth Encore Worsted medium (worsted) weight acrylic/wool yarn (3½ oz/200 yds/100g per ball):
  2 yds #470 French vanilla (A)
  1 yd #458 purple orchid (B)
- Size I/9/5.5mm crochet hook or size needed to obtain gauge
- Tapestry needle

GAUGE

Motif = 4 inches (blocked)

Take time to check gauge.

PATTERN NOTES

Weave in ends as work progresses.

Join with slip stitch as indicated unless otherwise stated.

Chain-3 at beginning of round or row counts as a double crochet unless otherwise stated.

Chain-4 at beginning of round or row counts as a double crochet and chain-1 space unless otherwise stated.

SPECIAL STITCHES

Beginning shell (beg shell): Ch 4 (see Pattern Notes), [dc, ch 1] 3 times in indicated sp, dc in same st or sp.

Shell: [Dc, ch 1] 4 times in indicated sp, dc in same st or sp.

MOTIF

Rnd 1 (RS): With A, ch 4, **join** (see Pattern Notes) in first ch to form ring, **ch 3** (see Pattern Notes), 11 dc in ring, join in 3rd ch of beg ch-3. (12 dc)

Rnd 2: Ch 1, (sc, ch 7, sc) in same ch as beg ch-1, sc in each of next 2 sts, *(sc, ch 7, sc) in next st, sc in each of next 2 sts, rep from * twice, join in first sc. (16 sc, 4 ch-7 sps)

Rnd 3: Sl st in each of next 2 chs of next ch-7 sp, **beg shell** (see Special Stitches) in same sp, *ch 1, sk next st, **dc dec** (see Stitch Guide) in next 2 sts, ch 1, sk next st, **shell** (see Special Stitches) in next ch-7 sp, rep from * twice, ch 1, sk next st, dc dec in next 2 sts, ch 1, sk next st, join in 3rd ch of beg ch-4. Fasten off. (4 shells, 4 dc)

Rnd 4: Join B with sc in same ch as joining, sc in next ch-1 sp, sc in next st, sc in next ch-1 sp, *(sc, ch 5, sc) in next st, sc in each of next 11 chs and sts, rep from * twice, (sc, ch 5, sc) in next st, sc in each of last 7 sts and sps, join in first sc. Fasten off. *(52 sc, 4 ch-5 sps)*

HALF MOTIF

Row 1 (RS): With A, ch 4, **join** *(see Pattern Notes)* in first ch to form ring, **ch 3** *(see Pattern Notes)*, 6 dc in ring, turn. *(7 dc)*

Row 2 (WS): Ch 1, (sc, ch 7, sc) in first st, sc in each of next 2 sts, (sc, ch 7, sc) in next st, sc in each of next 2 sts, (sc, ch 7, sc) in last st, turn. *(10 sc, 3 ch-7 sps)*

Row 3: Sl st in each of first 3 chs of next ch-7 sp, **ch 4** *(see Pattern Notes)*, (dc, ch 1, dc) in same sp, ch 1, sk next st, **dc dec** *(see Stitch Guide)* in next 2 sts, ch 1, sk next st, **shell** *(see Special Stitches)* in next ch-7 sp, ch 1, sk next st, dc dec in next 2 sts, ch 1, sk next st, ([dc, ch 1] twice, dc) in last ch-7 sp. Fasten off.

Row 4: With RS facing, join B with sc in 3rd ch of beg ch-4, ch 5, sc in same sc, sc in each of next 11 sts and chs, (sc, ch 5, sc) in next st, sc in each of next 11 sts and chs, (sc, ch 5, sc) in last st. Fasten off. ∎

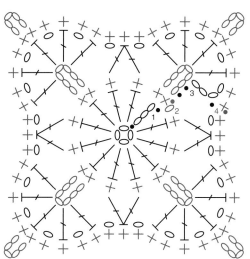

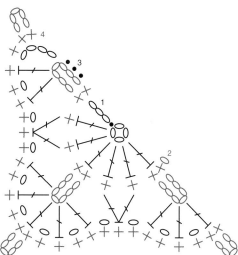

Star Square
Motif Stitch Diagram

Star Square
Half Motif Stitch Diagram

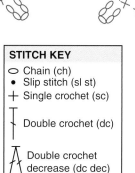

STITCH KEY
⟠ Chain (ch)
• Slip stitch (sl st)
+ Single crochet (sc)

Ŧ Double crochet (dc)

Ѧ Double crochet decrease (dc dec)

Target Square

SKILL LEVEL

BEGINNER

FINISHED MEASUREMENTS
Motif: 5 inches x 5 inches

Half Motif: 6 inches x 3½ inches

MATERIALS
- Plymouth Encore Worsted medium (worsted) weight acrylic/wool yarn (3½ oz/200 yds/100g per ball):
  - 4 yds #469 storm blue (A)
  - 1 yd #473 aquarius (B)
- Size J/10/6mm crochet hook or size needed to obtain gauge
- Tapestry needle

GAUGE
Motif = 5 inches (blocked)

Take time to check gauge.

PATTERN NOTES
Weave in ends as work progresses.

Join with slip stitch as indicated unless otherwise stated.

Chain-4 at beginning of round counts as a treble crochet unless otherwise stated.

Chain-3 at beginning of row counts as a double crochet unless otherwise stated.

MOTIF
Rnd 1 (RS): With A, ch 5, **join** (see Pattern Notes) in first ch to form ring, **ch 4** (see Pattern Notes), 15 tr in ring, join in 4th ch of beg ch-4. Fasten off. (16 tr)

Rnd 2: Working in **back lps** (see Stitch Guide), join B with dc in any st, dc in same st, 2 dc in each rem st around, join in first dc. Fasten off. (32 dc)

Rnd 3: Working in back lps, join A with dc in any st, dc in each of next 7 sts, ch 5, *dc in each of next 8 sts, ch 5, rep from * twice, join in first dc. (32 dc, 4 ch-5 sps)

Rnd 4: Working through both lps, ch 1, sc in same st as beg ch-1, sc in each of next 7 sts, (3 sc, ch 3, 3 sc) in next ch-5 sp, *sc in each of next 8 sts, (3 sc, ch 3, 3 sc) in next ch-5 sp, rep from * twice, join in first sc. Fasten off. (*56 sc, 4 ch-3 sps*)

HALF MOTIF
Row 1 (RS): With A, ch 5, **join** (*see Pattern Notes*) in first ch to form ring, **ch 3** (*see Pattern Notes*), 8 dc in ring. Fasten off. (*9 dc*)

Row 2: With RS facing and working in **back lps** (*see Stitch Guide*), join B with dc in first st, dc in same st, 2 dc in each rem st across. Fasten off. (*18 dc*)

Row 3: With RS facing and working in back lps, join A with dc in first st, ch 3, dc in each of next 8 sts, ch 5, dc in each of next 8 sts, ch 3, dc in last st, turn (*18 dc, 2 ch-3 sps, 1 ch-5 sp*)

Row 4: Ch 3, 3 sc in next ch-3 sp, sc in each of next 8 sts, (3 sc, ch 3, 3 sc) in next ch-5 sp, sc in each of next 8 sts, 3 sc in next ch-3 sp, ch 3, sl st in last st. Fasten off. (*28 sc, 2 ch-3 sps, 1 ch-5 sp*) ∎

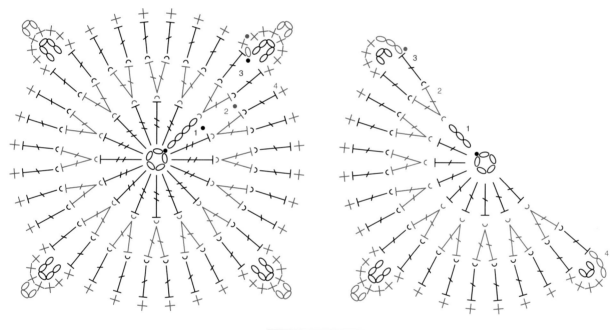

Target Square
Motif Stitch Diagram

Target Square
Half Motif Stitch Diagram

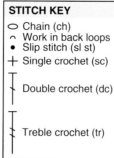

STITCH KEY
◯ Chain (ch)
∩ Work in back loops
● Slip stitch (sl st)
+ Single crochet (sc)

⊤ Double crochet (dc)

⊤ Treble crochet (tr)

Tracing Square

SKILL LEVEL

EASY

FINISHED MEASUREMENTS
Motif: 6 inches x 6 inches

Half Motif: 7 inches x 4 inches

MATERIALS
- Plymouth Encore Worsted medium (worsted) weight acrylic/wool yarn (3½ oz/200 yds/100g per ball):
  6 yds #461 living coral
- Size I/9/5.5mm crochet hook or size needed to obtain gauge
- Tapestry needle

GAUGE
Motif = 6 inches x 6 inches (blocked)

Take time to check gauge.

PATTERN NOTES
Join with slip stitch as indicated unless otherwise stated.

Chain-4 at beginning of round or row counts as a treble crochet unless otherwise stated.

Chain-3 at beginning of round or row counts as a double crochet unless otherwise stated.

MOTIF
Rnd 1 (RS): Ch 4, **join** (see Pattern Notes) in first ch to form ring, **ch 4** (see Pattern Notes), 15 tr in ring, join in 4th ch of beg ch-4. (16 tr)

Rnd 2: Ch 1, (sc, ch 15, sc) in same st as beg ch-1, (sc, ch 15, sc) in next st, (sc, ch 11, sc) in each of next 2 sts, *(sc, ch 15, sc) in each of next 2 sts, (sc, ch 11, sc) in each of next 2 sts, rep from * around, join in first sc. (8 ch-15 sps, 8 ch-11 sps)

Rnd 3: Sl st in each of next 7 chs of next ch-15 sp, ch 1, 3 sc in ch-15 sp, ch 3 (corner sp made), 3 sc in next ch-15 sp, ch 1, [2 sc in next ch-11 sp, ch 1] twice, *3 sc in next ch-15 sp, ch 3 (corner sp made), 3 sc in next ch-15 sp, ch 1, [2 sc in next ch-11 sp, ch 1] twice, rep from * twice, join in first sc. (40 sc, 4 ch-3 corner sps)

Rnd 4: Ch 3 (see Pattern Notes), dc in each of next 2 sts, (2 dc, ch 3, 2 dc) in next corner ch-3 sp, *dc in each st and ch across to next ch-3 corner sp, (2 dc, ch 3, 2 dc) in ch-3 corner sp, rep from * twice, dc in each st and each ch across to beg ch-3, join in 3rd ch of beg ch-3. Fasten off. (68 dc, 4 ch-3 sps)

HALF MOTIF

Row 1 (WS): Ch 4, **join** *(see Pattern Notes)* in first ch to form ring, **ch 4** *(see Pattern Notes)*, 8 tr in ring, turn. *(9 tr)*

Row 2 (RS): Ch 12, sl st in 5th ch from hook and in each rem ch to first ch, sc in first st, *(sc, ch 15, sc) in next st, (sc, ch 11, sc) in each of next 2 sts, (sc, ch 15, sc) in each of next 2 sts, (sc, ch 11, sc) in each of next 2 sts, (sc, ch 15, sc) in next st, ch 12, sl st in 5th ch from hook and in each rem ch to first ch. Fasten off.

Row 3: With WS facing, join with sc in first ch-5 sp, ch 3, 3 sc in next ch-15 sp, ch 1, [2 sc in next ch-11 sp, ch 1] twice, 3 sc in next ch-15 sp, ch 3, 3 sc in next ch-15 sp, ch 1, [2 sc in next ch-11 sp, ch 1] twice, 3 sc in next ch-15 sp, ch 3, sc in last ch-5 sp, turn.

Row 4: Ch 3 *(see Pattern Notes)*, (dc, ch 3, 2 dc) in next ch-3 sp, [dc in each st and ch across to next ch-3 sp, (2 dc, ch 3, 2 dc) in next ch-3 sp] twice. Fasten off. ■

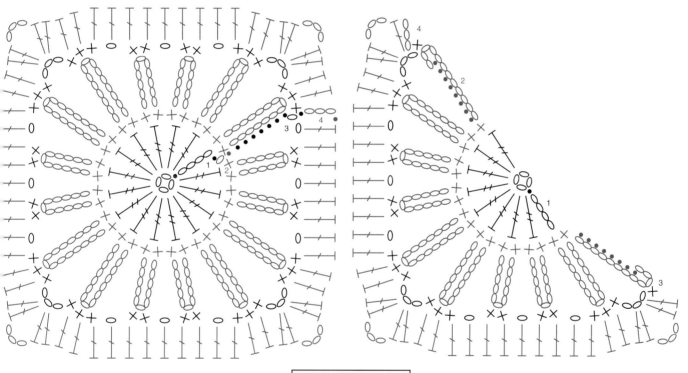

Tracing Square
Motif Stitch Diagram

STITCH KEY
⬭ Chain (ch)
● Slip stitch (sl st)
+ Single crochet (sc)
⊤ Double crochet (dc)
⊥ Treble crochet (tr)

Tracing Square
Half Motif Stitch Diagram

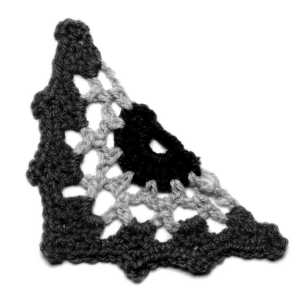

First 20 Minutes

SKILL LEVEL

EASY

FINISHED MEASUREMENTS

Motif: 7 inches across

Half Motif: 7 inches x 3 inches

MATERIALS

- Plymouth Encore Worsted medium (worsted) weight acrylic/wool yarn (3½ oz/200 yds/100g per ball):
    4 yds #453 rust roadster (A)
    2 yds each #149 periwinkle heather (B) and #555 Bristol wedgewood (C)
- Size J/10/6mm crochet hook or size needed to obtain gauge
- Tapestry needle

GAUGE

Motif = 7 inches across (blocked)

Take time to check gauge.

PATTERN NOTES

Weave in ends as work progresses.

Join with slip stitch as indicated unless otherwise stated.

Chain-3 at beginning of round or row counts as a double crochet unless otherwise stated.

MOTIF

Rnd 1 (RS): With C, ch 10, **join** (*see Pattern Notes*) in first ch to form ring, **ch 3** (*see Pattern Notes*), 23 dc in ring, join in 3rd ch of beg ch-3. Fasten off. (*24 dc*)

Rnd 2: Join B with sc in any st, ch 3, sk next st, *sc in next sc, ch 3, sk next st, rep from * around, join in first sc. (*12 sc, 12 ch-3 sps*)

Rnd 3: Sl st in next ch-3 sp, sc in same sp, ch 5, *sc in next ch-3 sp, ch 5, rep from * around, join in first sc. Fasten off. (*12 sc, 12 ch-5 sps*)

Rnd 4: Join A with dc in any ch-5 sp, 4 dc in same sp, *ch 1, [3 dc in next ch-5 sp, ch 1] twice, 5 dc in next ch-5 sp, rep from * twice, [ch 1, 3 dc in next ch-5 sp] twice, ch 1, join in first dc. (*44 dc, 9 ch-1 sps*)

Rnd 5: Ch 1, sc in same dc as beg ch-1 and in next dc, *(sc, ch 3, sc) in next st, sc in each of next 2 sts, sc in next ch-1 sp, [sc in next st, (sc, ch 3, sc) in next st, sc in next st, sc in next ch-1 sp] twice**, sc in each of next 2 sts, rep from * around, ending last rep at **, join in first sc. Fasten off. (*68 sc, 12 ch-3 sps*)

HALF MOTIF

Row 1 (RS): With C, ch 7, **join** (see Pattern Notes) in first ch to form ring, **ch 3** (see Pattern Notes), 12 dc in ring. Fasten off. (13 dc)

Row 2: With WS facing, join B with sc in first st, *ch 3, sk next st, sc in next st, rep from * across, turn. (7 sc, 6 ch-3 sps)

Row 3: Ch 5, sc in next ch-3 sp, ch 5, [sc in next ch-3 sp, ch 5] 5 times, sc in last st, turn. Fasten off. (7 sc, 7 ch-5 sps)

Row 4: With WS facing, join A with dc in first ch-5 sp, 2 dc in same sp, ch 1, [3 dc in next ch-5 sp, ch 1] twice, 5 dc in next ch-5 sp, [ch 1, 3 dc in next ch-5 sp] 3 times, turn. (23 dc, 6 ch-1 sps)

Row 5: Ch 1, (sc, ch 3, sc) in first st, sc in each of next 2 sts, [sc in next ch-1 sp, sc in next st, (sc, ch 3, sc) in next st, sc in next st] twice, sc in next ch-1 sp, sc in each of next 2 sts, (sc, ch 3, sc) in next st, sc in each of next 2 sts, [sc in next ch-1 sp, sc in next st, (sc, ch 3, sc) in next st, sc in next st] twice, sc in next ch-1 sp, sc in each of next 2 sts, (sc, ch 3, sc) in last st. Fasten off. (33 sc, 6 ch-3 sps) ■

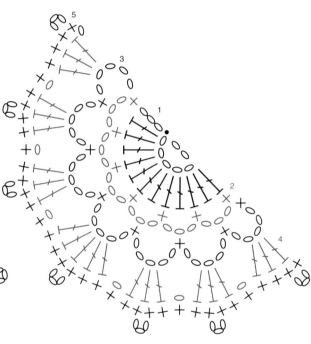

First 20 Minutes
Half Motif Stitch Diagram

First 20 Minutes
Motif Stitch Diagram

STITCH KEY

◯ Chain (ch)
● Slip stitch (sl st)
+ Single crochet (sc)

Ⴌ Double crochet (dc)

Second 20 Minutes

SKILL LEVEL

INTERMEDIATE

FINISHED MEASUREMENTS

Motif: 7 inches x 7 inches (side to side)

Half Motif: 7 inches wide x 4 inches tall

MATERIALS

- Plymouth Encore Worsted medium (worsted) weight acrylic/wool yarn (3½ oz/200 yds/100g per ball):
  8 yds #959 mauvetone (A)
  4 yds #461 living coral (B)
- Size J/10/6mm crochet hook or size needed to obtain gauge
- Tapestry needle

GAUGE

Motif = 7 inches x 7 inches (blocked)

Take time to check gauge.

PATTERN NOTES

Weave in ends as work progresses.

Join with slip stitch as indicated unless otherwise stated.

Chain-4 at beginning of round counts as a treble crochet unless otherwise stated.

SPECIAL STITCHES

Beginning treble crochet cluster (beg tr cl): Ch 4 (*see Pattern Notes*), holding back last lp of each st on hook, 2 tr in same sp as beg ch-4, yo and draw through 3 lps on hook.

Treble crochet cluster (tr cl): Holding back last lp of each st on hook, 3 tr in indicated sp, yo and draw through 4 lps on hook.

Double crochet cluster (dc cl): Holding back last lp of each st on hook, 3 dc in indicated sp, yo and draw through 4 lps on hook.

MOTIF

Rnd 1 (RS): With B, ch 4, **join** (*see Pattern Notes*) in first ch to form ring, **beg tr cl** (*see Special Stitches*) in ring, ch 3, [**tr cl** (*see Special Stitches*) in ring, ch 3] 5 times, join in top of beg tr cl. Fasten off. (*6 tr cls, 6 ch-3 sps*)

Rnd 2: Join A with dc in any tr cl, 4 dc in next ch-3 sp, *dc in next tr cl, 4 dc in next ch-3 sp, rep from * 4 times, join in first dc. Fasten off. (*30 dc*)

Rnd 3: Join B with dc in any dc, **fpdc** (*see Stitch Guide*) around post of same st, [dc in next st, fpdc around post of same st] around, join in first dc. Fasten off. (*30 dc, 30 fpdc*)

Rnd 4: Join A with tr in fpdc above any tr cl on rnd 1, *[ch 1, sk next dc, **dc cl** (*see Special Stitches*) in next fpdc] 4 times, ch 1**, (tr, ch 3, tr) in next st, rep from * 5 times, ending last rep at **, tr in same st as first tr worked, ch 3, join in first tr. *(24 dc cls, 12 tr, 6 ch-3 sps)*

Rnd 5: Ch 1, sc in same st as beg ch-1, ch 5, *sk next dc cl, sc in ch-1 sp between next 2 dc cls, ch 5, sc in next tr, ch 5**, sc in next tr, rep from * around, ending last rep at **, join in first sc. Fasten off.

HALF MOTIF
Row 1 (RS): With B, ch 4, **join** *(see Pattern Notes)* in first ch to form ring, **beg tr cl**

(see Special Stitches) in ring, [ch 3, **tr cl**—*see Special Stitches*] 3 times in ring. Fasten off. *(4 tr cls, 3 ch-3 sps)*

Row 2: With WS facing, join A with dc in first tr cl, [4 dc in next ch-3 sp, dc in next tr cl] 3 times. Fasten off. *(16 dc)*

Row 3: With RS facing, join B with dc in first st, **fpdc** *(see Stitch Guide)* around post of same st, [dc in next st, fpdc around post of same st] across. Fasten off. *(16 dc, 16 fpdc)*

Row 4: With WS facing, join A with tr in first st, *ch 3, tr in same st, ch 1, sk next st, [**dc cl**—*see Special Stitches* in next st, ch 1, sk next st] 3 times, dc cl in next st, ch 1, sk next st, tr in next st, rep from * twice, ch 3, tr in same st, turn. *(12 dc cls, 8 tr, 4 ch-3 sps)*

Row 5: Ch 1, sc in first tr, ch 5, sc in next tr, ch 5, sk next dc cl, sc in ch-1 sp between next 2 dc cls, ch 5, *sc in next tr, ch 5, sc in next tr, ch 5, sk next dc cl, sc in ch-1 sp between next 2 dc cls, ch 5, rep from * once, sc in next tr, ch 5, sc in last tr. Fasten off. ∎

STITCH KEY
◯ Chain (ch)
• Slip stitch (sl st)
+ Single crochet (sc)
Double crochet (dc)
Treble crochet (tr)
Front post double crochet (fpdc)
Beginning double crochet cluster (beg dc cl)
Double crochet cluster (dc cl)
Beginning treble crochet cluster (beg tr cl)
Treble crochet cluster (tr cl)

Second 20 Minutes
Motif Stitch Diagram

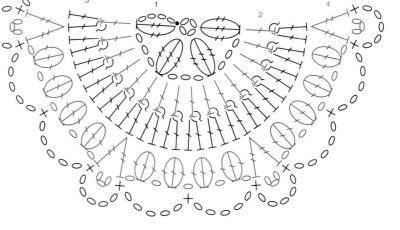

Second 20 Minutes
Half Motif Stitch Diagram

Two-Tone Coral Hexagon

SKILL LEVEL

INTERMEDIATE

FINISHED MEASUREMENTS

Motif: 4½ inches x 4½ inches (side to side)

Half Motif: 5½ inches wide x 2¾ inches tall

MATERIALS

- Plymouth Encore Worsted medium (worsted) weight acrylic/wool yarn (3½ oz/200 yds/100g per ball):
    4 yds each #461 living coral (A) and #453 rust roadster (B)
- Size J/10/6mm crochet hook or size needed to obtain gauge
- Tapestry needle

MEDIUM 4

GAUGE

Motif = 4½ inches (blocked)

Take time to check gauge.

PATTERN NOTES

Weave in ends as work progresses.

Join with slip stitch as indicated unless otherwise stated.

Chain-7 at beginning of round or row counts as a double crochet and chain-4 space unless otherwise stated.

SPECIAL STITCHES

Beginning cluster (beg cl): Ch 3, holding back last lp of each st on hook, 2 dc in same st as beg ch-3, yo and draw through 3 lps on hook.

Cluster (cl): Holding back last lp of each st on hook, 3 dc in indicated st, yo and draw through 4 lps on hook.

MOTIF

Rnd 1 (RS): With A, ch 5, **join** (see Pattern Notes) in first ch to form ring, ch 1, 12 sc in ring, join in first sc. (12 sc)

Rnd 2: Ch 7 (see Pattern Notes), sk next st, [dc in next st, ch 4, sk next st] 5 times, join in 3rd ch of beg ch-7. Fasten off. (6 dc, 6 ch-4 sps)

Rnd 3: Join B in any st, (**beg cl**—see Special Stitches, ch 3, **cl**—see Special Stitches) in same st as joining, *ch 3, sc in next ch-4 sp, ch 3, (cl, ch 3, cl) in next st, rep from * 4 times, ch 3, sc in next ch-4 sp, ch 3, join in top of beg cl. Fasten off. (12 cls, 6 sc, 18 ch-3 sps)

Rnd 4: Join A with sc in ch-3 sp between any 2 cls, ch 5, sc in same sp, *ch 4, sk next cl, dc in next sc, ch 4, (sc, ch 5, sc) in ch-3 sp between next 2 cls, rep from * 4 times, ch 4, sk next cl, dc in next sc, ch 4, join in first sc. Fasten off. (*6 dc, 6 ch-5 sps, 12 ch-4 sps*)

HALF MOTIF

Row 1 (RS): With A, ch 5, **join** (*see Pattern Notes*) in first ch to form ring, ch 1, 7 sc in ring, turn (*7 sc*)

Row 2: Ch 7 (*see Pattern Notes*), sk next st, dc in next st, [ch 4, sk next st, dc in next st] twice. Fasten off. (*4 dc, 3 ch-4 sps*)

Row 3: With RS facing, join B with dc in first st, ch 3, cl in same st, *ch 3, sc in next ch-4 sp, ch 3, (cl, ch 3, cl) in next st, rep from * once, ch 3, sc in next ch-4 sp, ch 3, cl in next ch-4 sp, ch 3, dc in last st. Fasten off. (*6 cls, 2 dc, 2 sc*)

Row 4: With WS facing, join A with sc in first ch-3 sp, ch 5, sc in same ch-3 sp, *ch 4, dc in next sc, ch 4, sk next ch-3 sp, (sc, ch 5, sc) in next ch-3 sp, rep from * once, ch 4, dc in next sc, ch 4, sk next ch-3 sp, (sc, ch 5, sc) in last ch-3 sp. Fasten off. (*3 dc, 4 ch-5 sps, 6 ch-4 sps*) ■

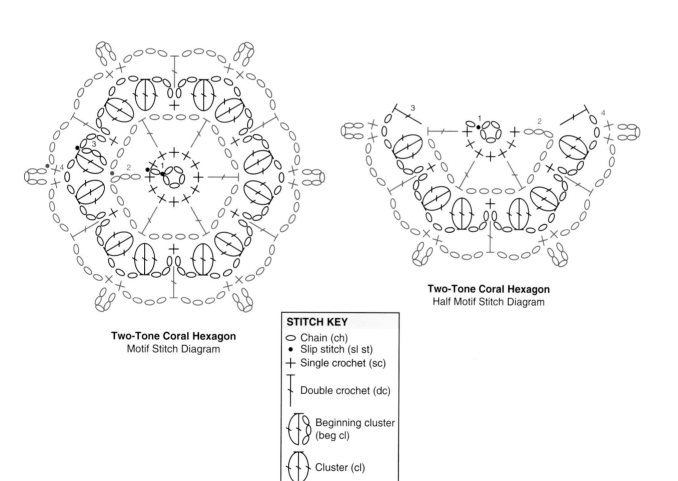

Two-Tone Coral Hexagon
Motif Stitch Diagram

Two-Tone Coral Hexagon
Half Motif Stitch Diagram

STITCH KEY
⌒ Chain (ch)
• Slip stitch (sl st)
+ Single crochet (sc)

⊤ Double crochet (dc)

Beginning cluster (beg cl)

Cluster (cl)

Blossom Hexagon

SKILL LEVEL

INTERMEDIATE

FINISHED MEASUREMENTS
Motif: 6 inches across

Half Motif: 6 inches wide x 3 inches tall

MATERIALS

- Plymouth Encore Worsted medium (worsted) weight acrylic/wool yarn (3½ oz/200 yds/100g per ball):
  5 yds #1308 beach berry (A)
  3 yds #1606 purple bell (B)
  1 yd #470 French vanilla (C)
- Size J/10/6mm crochet hook or size needed to obtain gauge
- Tapestry needle

GAUGE
Motif = 6 inches across (blocked)

Take time to check gauge.

PATTERN NOTES
Weave in ends as work progresses.

Join with slip stitch as indicated unless otherwise stated.

Chain-3 at beginning of round or row counts as a double crochet unless otherwise stated.

Chain-5 at beginning of row counts as a double crochet and chain-2 space unless otherwise stated.

MOTIF
Rnd 1 (RS): With C, ch 4, **join** (see Pattern Notes) in first ch to form ring, **ch 3** (see Pattern Notes), 11 dc in ring, join in 3rd ch of beg ch-3. Fasten off. (12 dc)

Rnd 2: Join A with sc in any st, **fpdc** (see Stitch Guide) around post of same st, [sc in next dc, fpdc around post of same st] 11 times, join in first sc. (12 fpdc, 12 sc)

Rnd 3: Ch 1, sc in same st as beg ch-1, ch 5, sk next st, *sc in next st, ch 5, sk next st, rep from * around, join in first sc. Fasten off. (12 sc, 12 ch-5 sps)

Rnd 4: Working behind ch-5 sps, join B with tr in any fpdc on rnd 2, 2 tr in same st, ch 1, *3 tr in next fpdc, ch 1, rep from * around, join in first tr. Fasten off. (36 tr, 12 ch-1 sps)

Rnd 5: Join A with sc in any ch-1 sp, *sc in next tr, sc through next ch-5 sp on rnd 3 and next tr on working rnd at same time, sc in next tr**, sc in next ch-1 sp, rep from * around, ending last rep at **, join in first sc. (48 sc)

Rnd 6: Sl st in each of next 2 sts, ch 3, 4 dc in same st as last sl st made, *ch 1, sk next 3 sts, (dc, ch 5, dc) in next st, ch 1, sk next 3 sts**, 5 dc in next st, rep from * around, ending last rep at ** , join in 3rd ch of beg ch-3. Fasten off. (30 dc, 6 ch-5 sp, 12 ch-1 sps)

HALF MOTIF

Row 1 (RS): With C, ch 4, **join** (see Pattern Notes) in first ch to form ring, **ch 3** (see Pattern Notes), 7 dc in ring. Fasten off. (8 dc)

Row 2: With WS facing, join A with sc in first st, **bpdc** (see Stitch Guide) around post of same st, [sc in next st, bpdc around same st] 6 times, sc in last st, turn (8 sc, 7 bpdc)

Row 3: Ch 1, sc in first st, *ch 5, sk next st, sc in next st, rep from * 5 times. Fasten off. (8 sc, 7 ch-5 sps)

Row 4: With RS facing and working behind ch-5 sps, join B with tr in first bpdc on row 2, 2 tr in same st, *ch 1, 3 tr in next bpdc, rep from * across. Fasten off. (21 tr, 6 ch-1 sps)

Row 5: With WS facing, join A with sc in first st, *sc in next tr and in corresponding ch-5 sp on row 3 at same time, sc in next tr**, sc in next ch-1 sp, sc in next tr, rep from * across, ending last rep at **, turn (27 sc)

Row 6: Ch 5 (see Pattern Notes), dc in next st, *ch 1, sk next 3 sts, 5 dc in next st, ch 1, sk next 3 sts**, (dc, ch 5, dc) in next st, rep from * across, ending last rep at **, dc in next st, ch 2, dc in last st. Fasten off. (23 dc, 2 ch-5 sps) ■

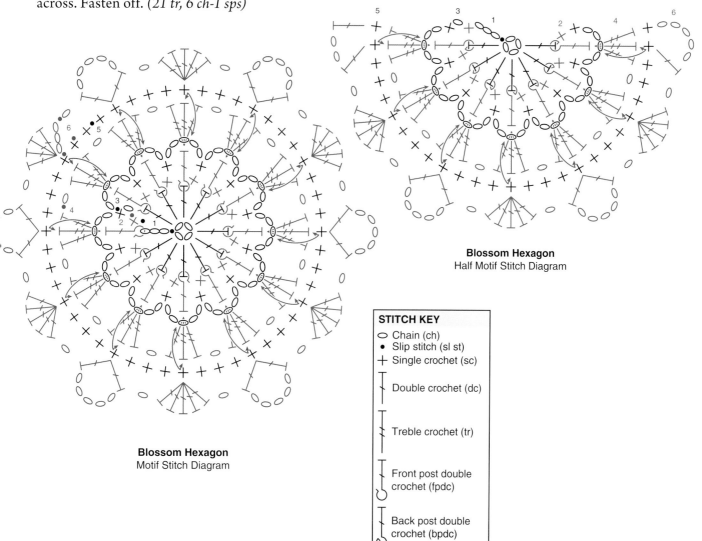

Blossom Hexagon
Half Motif Stitch Diagram

Blossom Hexagon
Motif Stitch Diagram

STITCH KEY
◯ Chain (ch)
• Slip stitch (sl st)
+ Single crochet (sc)

⊤ Double crochet (dc)

⊤ Treble crochet (tr)

⊥ Front post double crochet (fpdc)

⊥ Back post double crochet (bpdc)

Windy

SKILL LEVEL

EASY

FINISHED MEASUREMENTS

Motif: 5½ inches x 5½ inches (side to side)

Half Motif: 6 inches wide x 3 inches tall

MATERIALS

- Plymouth Encore Worsted medium (worsted) weight acrylic/wool yarn (3½ oz/200 yds/100g per ball):
  5 yds #149 periwinkle heather (A)
  3 yds #458 purple orchid (B)
  2 yds #256 ecru (C)
- Size I/9/5.5mm crochet hook or size needed to obtain gauge
- Tapestry needle

MEDIUM

GAUGE

Motif = 5½ inches x 5½ inches (blocked)

Take time to check gauge.

PATTERN NOTES

Weave in ends as work progresses.

Join with slip stitch as indicated unless otherwise stated.

Chain-9 at beginning of round or row counts as a double crochet and chain-6 space unless otherwise stated.

SPECIAL STITCHES

Beginning cluster (beg cl): Ch 3, holding back last lp of each st on hook, 2 dc in same place as beg ch-3, yo and draw through 3 lps on hook.

Cluster (cl): Holding back last lp of each st on hook, 3 dc as indicated in instructions, yo and draw through 4 lps on hook.

MOTIF

Rnd 1 (RS): With B, ch 4, **join** (see Pattern Notes) in first ch to form ring, **beg cl** (see Special Stitches), ch 4, [**cl** (see Special Stitches) in ring, ch 4] 5 times, join in beg cl. (6 cls, 6 ch-4 sps)

Rnd 2: Ch 9 (see Pattern Notes), *dc in next cl, ch 6, rep from * around, join in 3rd ch of beg ch-9. Fasten off. (6 dc, 6 ch-6 sps)

Rnd 3: Join A in same ch as joining, working in front of ch-6 sps, sk first ch-6 sp, (**dtr**—see Stitch Guide, tr, dc, hdc, sc) around post of each of next 5 dc, (dtr, tr, dc, hdc, sc) around beg 3 chs of beg ch-9, join in first dtr. Fasten off. (6 dtr, 6 tr, 6 dc, 6 hdc, 6 sc)

Rnd 4: Working in **back lps** (see Stitch Guide), join C with dc in same st as joining, dc in each of next 3 sts, *5 dc in next st, **dc in each of next 4 sts, rep from * around, 5 dc in last st, join in first dc. Fasten off. (54 dc)

Rnd 5: Join B with sc in 3rd dc of any 5-dc group, 2 sc in same st, *sc in each of next 8 sts, 3 sc in next st, rep from * 5 times, sc in each of next 8 sts, join in first sc. Fasten off. *(66 sc)*

Rnd 6: Working behind rnd 5, join A with tr in any ch-6 sp on rnd 2, 8 tr in same sp, 3 sc in 2nd sc of next 3-sc group on rnd 5, *9 tr in next ch-6 sp on rnd 2, 3 sc in 2nd sc of next 3-sc group on rnd 5, rep from * around, join in first sc. Fasten off. *(54 tr, 18 sc)*

HALF MOTIF

Row 1 (RS): With B, ch 4, **join** *(see Pattern Notes)* in first ch to form ring, **beg cl** *(see Special Stitches)* in ring, [ch 4, **cl** *(see Special Stitches)* in ring] 3 times, turn. *(4 cls, 3 ch-4 sps)*

Row 2: Ch 9 *(see Pattern Notes)*, [dc in next cl, ch 6] twice, dc in last cl. Fasten off. *(4 dc, 3 ch-6 sps)*

Row 3: With RS facing, join A with sc around post of first st, 3 sc around post of same st, (**dtr**—*see Stitch Guide*, tr, dc, hdc, sc) around post of each of next 3 dc. Fasten off. *(3 dtr, 3 tr, 3 dc, 3 hdc, 7 sc)*

Row 4: With RS facing and working in **back lps** *(see Stitch Guide)*, join C with dc in first st, 2 dc in same st, dc in each of next 4 sts, *5 dc in next st, dc in each of next 4 sts, rep from * once, dc in each of next 4 sts, 3 dc in last st. Fasten off. *(28 dc)*

Row 5: With RS facing, join B with sc in first st, sc in same st, sc in each of next 8 sts, [3 sc in next st, sc in each of next 8 sts] twice, 2 sc in last st. Fasten off. *(34 sc)*

Row 6: With RS facing, join A with sc in first st, sc in same st, [working behind sts on working row, 9 tr in next ch-6 sp on row 2, 3 sc in 2nd sc of next 3-sc group on working row] twice, working behind sts on working row, 9 tr in next ch-6 sp on row 2, 2 sc in last sc on working row. Fasten off. ■

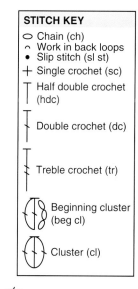

STITCH KEY

⬮ Chain (ch)
⌃ Work in back loops
● Slip stitch (sl st)
+ Single crochet (sc)
⊤ Half double crochet (hdc)
Double crochet (dc)
Treble crochet (tr)
Beginning cluster (beg cl)
Cluster (cl)

Windy Hexagon
Motif Stitch Diagram

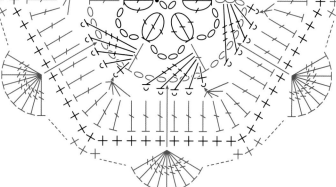

Windy Hexagon
Half Motif Stitch Diagram

Plus Square

SKILL LEVEL

INTERMEDIATE

FINISHED MEASUREMENTS

Motif: 6¾ inches x 6¾ inches (side to side)

Half Motif: 7½ inches x 4 inches

MATERIALS

- Plymouth Encore Worsted medium (worsted) weight acrylic/wool yarn (3½ oz/200 yds/100g per ball): 4 yds each #461 living coral (A) and #470 French vanilla (B)
- Size J/10/6mm crochet hook or size needed to obtain gauge
- Tapestry needle

GAUGE

Motif = 6¾ inches x 6¾ inches (blocked)

Take time to check gauge.

PATTERN NOTES

Weave in ends as work progresses.

Join with slip stitch as indicated unless otherwise stated.

Chain-3 at beginning of round counts as a double crochet unless otherwise stated.

Rnd 1 (RS): With A, ch 4, **join** (see Pattern Notes) in first ch to form ring, ch 1, 8 sc in ring, join in first sc. (8 sc)

Rnd 2: Ch 1, (sc, ch 7, sc) in same st as beg ch-1, ch 3, sk next st, *(sc, ch 7, sc) in next st, ch 3, sk next st, rep from * twice, join in first sc. (4 ch-3 sps, 4 ch-7 sps)

Rnd 3: Sl st in next ch-7 sp, **ch 3** (see Pattern Notes), 8 dc in same sp, ch 1, sc in next ch-3 sp, ch 1, *9 dc in next ch-7 sp, ch 1, sc in next ch-3 sp, ch 1, rep from * around, join in 3rd ch of beg ch-3. Fasten off. (36 dc, 4 sc)

Rnd 4: Join B with **dtr** (see Stitch Guide) in any sc, 6 dtr in same st, *ch 3, sc in 5th dc of next 9-dc group, ch 3**, 7 dtr in next sc, rep from * around, ending last rep at **, join in first dtr. (28 dtr, 4 sc, 8 ch-3 sps)

Rnd 5: Ch 1, sc in same st as beg ch-1, sc in each of next 2 sts, *(sc, ch 3, sc) in 4th dtr of next 7-dtr group (corner made), sc in each of next 3 dtr, 3 sc in next ch-3 sp, sc in next sc, 3 sc in next ch-3 sp**, sc in each of next 3 sts, rep from * around, ending last rep at **, join in first sc. Fasten off. (60 sc, 4 ch-3 sps)

Rnd 6: Join A with dc in any ch-3 corner sp, *dc in each st across to next ch-3 corner sp**, (dc, ch 3, dc) in ch-3 sp, rep from * around, ending last rep at **, dc in last ch-3 sp, ch 3, join in first dc. Fasten off. (68 dc, 4 ch-3 sps)

HALF MOTIF

Row 1 (RS): With A, ch 4, **join** (see Pattern Notes) in first ch to form ring, ch 1, 5 sc in ring, turn. (5 sc)

Row 2: Ch 1, sc in first st, ch 3, (sc, ch 7, sc) in next st, ch 3, sk next st, (sc, ch 7, sc) in next st, ch 3, sc in last st, turn. (2 ch-7 sps, 3 ch-3 sps)

Row 3: Ch 1, sc in first st, ch 1, 9 dc in next ch-7 sp, ch 1, sc in next ch-3 sp, ch 1, 9 dc in next ch-7 sp, ch 1, sc in last st. Fasten off. (18 dc, 3 sc)

Row 4: With RS facing, join B with **dtr** (see Stitch Guide) in first sc, 3 dtr in same st, ch 3, sc in 5th dc of next 9-dc group, ch 3, 7 dtr in next sc, ch 3, sc in 5th dc of next 9-dc group, ch 3, 4 dtr in last sc, turn. (15 dtr, 2 sc, 4 ch-3 sps)

Row 5: Ch 1, (sc, ch 3, sc) in first st, sc in each of next 3 sts, 3 sc in next ch-3 sp, sc in next sc, 3 sc in next ch-3 sp, sc in each of next 3 sts, (sc, ch 3, sc) in next st, sc in each of next 3 sts, 3 sc in next ch-3 sp, sc in next sc, 3 sc in next ch-3 sp, sc in each of next 3 sts, (sc, ch 3, sc) in last st. Fasten off. (32 sc, 3 ch-3 sps)

Row 6: With RS facing, join A with dc in first ch-3 sp, ch 3, dc in same sp, [dc in each st across to next ch-3 sp, (dc, ch 3, dc) in ch-3 sp] twice. Fasten off. (36 dc, 3 ch-3 sps) ■

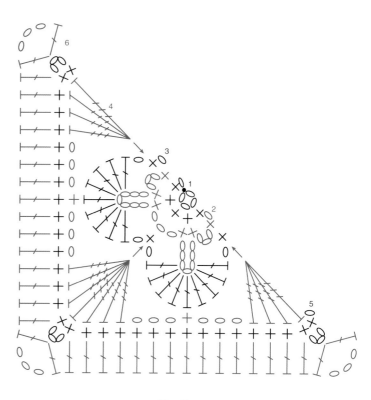

Plus Square
Half Motif Stitch Diagram

Plus Square
Motif Stitch Diagram

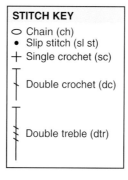

STITCH KEY
⬯ Chain (ch)
● Slip stitch (sl st)
+ Single crochet (sc)

Double crochet (dc)

Double treble (dtr)

Floating Square in a Square

SKILL LEVEL

EXPERIENCED

FINISHED MEASUREMENTS
Motif: 6¼ inches x 6¼ inches (side to side)

Half Motif: 7½ inches x 4½ inches

MATERIALS
- Plymouth Encore Worsted medium (worsted) weight acrylic/wool yarn (3½ oz/200 yds/100g per ball): 4 yds each #470 French vanilla (A) and #461 living coral (B)
- Size I/9/5.5mm crochet hook or size needed to obtain gauge
- Tapestry needle

GAUGE
Motif = 6¼ inches x 6¼ inches (blocked)

Take time to check gauge.

PATTERN NOTES
Weave in ends as work progresses.

Join with slip stitch as indicated unless otherwise stated.

Chain-7 at beginning of round or row counts as a double crochet and chain-4 space unless otherwise stated.

Chain-8 at beginning of round counts as a double crochet and chain-5 space unless otherwise stated.

Chain-5 at beginning of row counts as a double crochet and chain-2 space unless otherwise stated.

SPECIAL STITCHES
Cluster (cl): Holding back last lp of each st on hook, 3 dc in indicated sp, yo and draw through 4 lps on hook.

Beginning treble crochet cluster (beg tr cl): Ch 4, holding back last lp of each st on hook, 2 tr in same sp as beg ch-4, yo and draw through 3 lps on hook.

Treble crochet cluster (tr cl): Holding back last lp of each st on hook, 3 tr in indicated sp, yo and draw through 4 lps on hook.

Picot (picot): Ch 7, sl st in 7th ch from hook.

MOTIF
Rnd 1 (RS): With A, ch 4 **join** *(see Pattern Notes)* in first ch to form ring, **ch 7** *(see Pattern Notes)*, **cl** *(see Special Stitches)* in ring, ch 4, [dc in ring, ch 4, cl in ring, ch 4] 3 times, join in 3rd ch of beg ch-7. Fasten off. *(4 cls, 4 dc, 8 ch-4 sps)*

Rnd 2: Join B in any ch-4 sp before a cl, **beg tr cl** *(see Special Stitches)* in same sp, ch 4, *sc in next cl, ch 4, **tr cl** (see Special Stitches) in next ch-4 sp, **picot** (see Special Stitches), tr cl in next ch-4 sp, ch 4, rep from * twice, sc in next cl, ch 4, tr cl in next ch-4 sp, picot, join in beg tr cl. Fasten off. (8 tr cls, 8 ch-4 sps, 4 sc, 4 picots)

Rnd 3: Join A with sc in any picot, ch 3, sc in same picot, *ch 6, tr in next sc, ch 6**, (sc, ch 3, sc) in next picot, rep from * 3 times, ending last rep at **, join in first sc. (4 tr, 8 sc, 8 ch-6 sps, 4 ch-3 sps)

Rnd 4: Ch 8 (see Pattern Notes), dc in next st, *6 dc in next ch-6 sp, dc in next st, 6 dc in next ch-6 sp**, dc in next st, ch 5, dc in next st, rep from * 3 times, ending last rep at **, join in 3rd ch of beg ch-8. Fasten off. (60 dc, 4 ch-5 sps)

Rnd 5: Join A with sc in any ch-5 sp, (2 sc, hdc, 3 sc) in same sp, *sc in each dc across to next ch-5 sp, (3 sc, hdc, 3 sc) in ch-5 sp, rep from * twice, sc in each rem st to first sc, join in first sc. Fasten off.

HALF MOTIF
Row 1 (RS): With A, ch 4, **join** (see Pattern Notes) in first ch to form ring, **ch 7** (see Pattern Notes), **cl** (see Special Stitches) in ring, ch 4, dc in ring, ch 4, cl in ring, ch 4, dc in ring. Fasten off. (2 cls, 3 dc, 4 ch-4 sps)

Row 2: With RS facing, join B with tr in first ch-4 sp, **picot** (see Special Stitches), **tr cl** (see Special Stitches) in same sp, ch 4, sc in next cl, ch 4, tr cl in next ch-4 sp, picot, tr cl in next ch-4 sp, ch 4, sc in next cl, ch 4, tr cl in ch-4 sp, picot, tr in same sp. Fasten off. (4 tr cls, 2 tr, 2 sc, 4 ch-4 sps)

Row 3: With WS facing, join A with sc in first picot, ch 3, sc in same picot, ch 6, tr in next sc, ch 6, (sc, ch 3, sc) in next picot, ch 6, tr in next sc, ch 6, (sc, ch 3, sc) in last picot, turn. (6 sc, 2 tr, 4 ch-6 sps, 3 ch-3 sps)

Row 4: Ch 5 (see Pattern Notes), dc in next st, 6 dc in next ch-6 sp, dc in next st, 6 dc in next ch-6 sp, dc in next st, ch 5, dc in next st, 6 dc in next ch-5 sp, dc in next st, 6 dc in next ch-6 sp, dc in next st, ch 2, dc in last st. Fasten off. (32 dc)

Row 5: With RS facing, join B with hdc in first ch-2 sp, 3 sc in same sp, sc in each st to next ch-5 sp, (3 sc, hdc, 3 sc) in ch-5 sp, sc in each st across to next ch-2 sp, (3 sc, hdc) in ch-2 sp. Fasten off. (3 hdc, 42 sc) ■

STITCH KEY
- Chain (ch)
- Slip stitch (sl st)
- Single crochet (sc)
- Half double crochet (hdc)
- Double crochet (dc)
- Treble crochet (tr)
- Cluster (cl)
- Beginning treble crochet cluster (beg tr cl)
- Treble crochet cluster (tr cl)

Floating Square
Motif Stitch Diagram

Floating Square
Half Motif Stitch Diagram

Blanket Square

SKILL LEVEL

EASY

FINISHED MEASUREMENTS
Motif: 6 inches x 6 inches (side to side)

Half Motif: 7 inches wide x 3½ inches tall

MATERIALS
- Plymouth Encore Worsted medium (worsted) weight acrylic/wool yarn (3½ oz/200 yds/100g per ball):
  3 yds each #458 purple orchid (C) and #355 garnet mix (E)
  1 yd each #1385 bright fuchsia (A), #449 pink (B) and #514 light wedgewood (D)
- Size I/9/5.5mm crochet hook or size needed to obtain gauge
- Tapestry needle

GAUGE
Motif = 6 inches x 6 inches (blocked)

Take time to check gauge.

PATTERN NOTES
Weave in ends as work progresses

Join with slip stitch as indicated unless otherwise stated.

Chain-3 at beginning of round counts as a double crochet unless otherwise stated.

SPECIAL STITCHES
Beginning cluster (beg cl): Ch 3, holding back last lp of each st on hook, 2 dc in same st as beg ch-3, yo and draw through 3 lps on hook.

Cluster (cl): Holding back last lp of each st on hook, 3 dc in indicated st, yo and draw through 4 lps on hook.

MOTIF
Rnd 1 (RS): With A, ch 5, **join** (see Pattern Notes) in first ch to form ring, **ch 3** (see Pattern Notes), 15 dc in ring, join in 3rd ch of beg ch-3. Fasten off. (16 dc)

Rnd 2: Working in **back lps** (see Stitch Guide), join B with sc in any dc, sc in same st, 2 sc in each rem st around, join in first sc. Fasten off. (32 sc)

Rnd 3: Working through both lps, join C in same sc as joining, **beg cl** (see Special Stitches), ch 2, sk next st, *cl (see Special Stitches) in next st, ch 2, sk next st, rep from * 14 times, join in beg cl. (16 cls, 16 ch-2 sps)

Rnd 4: Ch 1, sc in same st as beg ch-1, 2 sc in next ch-2 sp, *sc in next cl, 2 sc in next ch-2 sp, rep around, join in first sc. Fasten off. (48 sc)

Rnd 5: Working in back lps, join D with sc in same sc as joining, sc in each rem st around, join in first sc. Fasten off.

Rnd 6: Working in back lps, join E with sc in same sc as joining, sc in same sc, sc in each of next 5 sts, *2 sc in next st, sc in each of next 5 sts, rep from * 6 times, join in first sc. *(56 sc)*

Rnd 7: Working through both lps, ch 3, dc in same st, ch 3 *(corner sp made)*, 2 dc in next st, hdc in next st, sc in each of next 10 sts, [hdc in next st, 2 dc in next st, ch 3 *(corner sp made)*, 2 dc in next st, hdc in next st, sc in next 10 sts] 3 times, hdc in next st, join in 3rd ch of beg ch-3. Fasten off. *(40 sc, 8 hdc, 16 dc, 4 ch-3 corner sps)*

HALF MOTIF

Row 1 (RS): With A, ch 5, **join** *(see Pattern Notes)* in first ch to form ring, **ch 3** *(see Pattern Notes)*, 8 dc in ring. Fasten off. *(9 dc)*

Row 2: With WS facing and working in **front lps** *(see Stitch Guide)*, join B with sc in first st, sc in same st, 2 sc in each rem st across. Fasten off. *(18 sc)*

Row 3: With RS facing, join C in first st, **beg cl** *(see Special Stitches)* in same st, *ch 2, sk next st, **cl** *(see Special Stitches)* in next st, rep from * across, leaving last sc unworked, turn. *(9 cls, 8 ch-2 sps)*

Row 4: Ch 1, sc in first st, 2 sc in next ch-2 sp, [sc in next st, 2 sc in next ch-2 sp] 7 times, sc in last st. Fasten off. *(25 sc)*

Row 5: With RS facing and working in **back lps** *(see Stitch Guide)*, join D with sc in first st, sc in each rem st across. Fasten off.

Row 6: With RS facing and working in back lps, join E with sc in first st, sc in each of next 5 sts, *2 sc in next st, sc in each of next 5 sts, rep from * twice, sc in last st, turn. *(28 sc)*

Row 7: Working through both lps, ch 1, sc in same st as beg ch-1, sc in each of next 4 sts, hdc in next st, 2 dc in next st, ch 3, 2 dc in next st, hdc in next st, sc in each of next 10 sts, hdc in next st, 2 dc in next st, ch 3, 2 dc in next st, hdc in next st, sc in next 5 sts. Fasten off. *(20 sc, 4 hdc, 8 dc, 2 ch-3 sps)* ∎

STITCH KEY	
⌒	Chain (ch)
⌃	Work in back loops
●	Slip stitch (sl st)
+	Single crochet (sc)
Ⱶ	Half double crochet (hdc)
Ⱶ	Double crochet (dc)
⬯	Beginning cluster (beg cl)
⬯	Cluster (cl)

Blanket Square
Motif Stitch Diagram

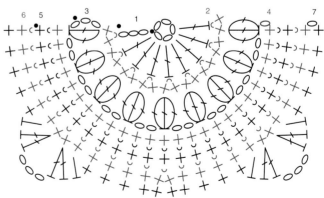

Blanket Square
Half Motif Stitch Diagram

Moody Hexagon

SKILL LEVEL

EASY

FINISHED MEASUREMENTS

Motif: 4½ inches across

Half Motif: 5½ inches wide x 2¾ inches tall

MATERIALS

- Plymouth Encore Worsted medium (worsted) weight acrylic/wool yarn (3½ oz/200 yds/100g per ball):
    4 yds #469 storm blue (A)
    3 yds #453 rust roadster (B)
    2 yds each #473 aquarius (C) and #1204 brownstone (D)
- Size J/10/6mm crochet hook or size needed to obtain gauge
- Tapestry needle

GAUGE

Motif = 4½ inches across (blocked)

Take time to check gauge.

PATTERN NOTES

Weave in ends as work progresses.

Join with slip stitch as indicated unless otherwise stated.

Chain-4 at beginning of round counts as a treble crochet unless otherwise stated.

Chain-6 at beginning of row counts as a treble crochet and chain-2 space unless otherwise stated.

MOTIF

Rnd 1 (RS): With C, ch 4, **join** *(see Pattern Notes)* in first ch to form ring, **ch 4** *(see Pattern Notes)*, 2 tr in ring, ch 2, [3 tr in ring, ch 2] 5 times, join in 4th ch of beg ch-4. Fasten off. *(18 tr, 6 ch-2 sps)*

Rnd 2: Join D with sc in any ch-2 sp, sc in same sp, sc in each of next 3 sts, *2 sc in next ch-2 sp, sc in each of next 3 sts, rep from * around, join in first sc. Fasten off. *(30 sc)*

Rnd 3: Join B with sc in first sc of any 2-sc group, *ch 3, sc in each of next 2 sts, **fpdc** *(see Stitch Guide)* around post of 2nd tr of next 3-tr group on rnd 1**, sc in each of next 2 sts on working rnd, rep from * around, ending last rep at **, sc in last st on working rnd, join in first sc. Fasten off. *(6 fpdc, 24 sc, 6 ch-3 sps)*

Rnd 4: Join A with dc in any ch-3 sp, 4 dc in same sp, *ch 2, fpdc around post of next fpdc, ch 2**, 5 dc in next ch-3 sp, rep from * around, ending last rep at ** , join in first dc. Fasten off. *(30 dc, 6 fpdc, 12 ch-2 sps)*

HALF MOTIF

Row 1 (RS): With C, ch 4, **join** *(see Pattern Notes)* in first ch to form ring, **ch 6** *(see Pattern Notes)*, [3 tr in ring, ch 2] 3 times, tr in ring. Fasten off. *(11 tr, 4 ch-2 sps)*

Row 2: With WS facing, join D with sc in first ch-2 sp, sc in same sp, [sc in each of next 3 sts, 2 sc in next ch-2 sp] 3 times. Fasten off. *(17 sc)*

Row 3: With RS facing, join B with sc in first st, ch 3, sc in next st, *sc in next st, **fpdc** *(see Stitch Guide)* around post of next tr on row 1, sc in each of next 2 sts, ch 3, sc in next st, rep from * twice. Fasten off.

Row 4: With RS facing, join A with dc in first ch-3 sp, 2 dc in same sp, *ch 2, fpdc around next fpdc, ch 2, 5 dc in next ch-3 sp, rep from * once, ch 2, fpdc around next fpdc, ch 2, 3 dc in last ch-3 sp. Fasten off. ∎

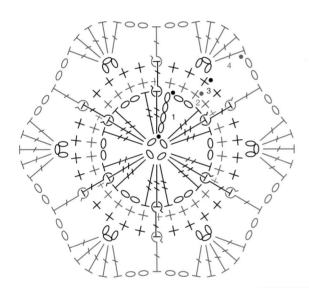

Moody Hexagon
Motif Stitch Diagram

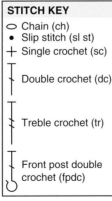

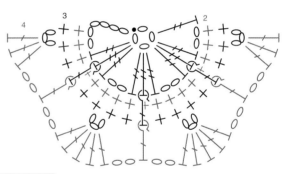

Moody Hexagon
Half Motif Stitch Diagram

STITCH KEY

◯ Chain (ch)
● Slip stitch (sl st)
+ Single crochet (sc)

┬ Double crochet (dc)

‡ Treble crochet (tr)

Front post double crochet (fpdc)

Mesh Hexagon

SKILL LEVEL

EASY

FINISHED MEASUREMENTS
Motif: 6 inches x 6 inches (side to side)

Half Motif: 7 inches wide x 3½ inches tall

MATERIALS
- Plymouth Encore Worsted medium (worsted) weight acrylic/wool yarn (3½ oz/200 yds/100g per ball):
  4 yds #137 California pink (A)
  3 yds #469 storm blue (B)
- Size J/10/6mm crochet hook or size needed to obtain gauge
- Tapestry needle

GAUGE
Motif = 6 inches x 6 inches (blocked)

Take time to check gauge.

PATTERN NOTES
Weave in ends as work progresses.

Join with slip stitch as indicated unless otherwise stated.

Chain-4 at beginning of round or row counts as a double crochet and chain-1 space unless otherwise stated.

Chain-5 at beginning of round or row counts as a double crochet and chain-2 space unless otherwise stated.

SPECIAL STITCH
V-stitch (V-st): (Dc, ch 2, dc) in indicated st or sp.

MOTIF
Rnd 1 (RS): With A, ch 5, **join** *(see Pattern Notes)* in first ch to form ring, **ch 4** *(see Pattern Notes)*, [dc in ring, ch 1] 11 times, join in 3rd ch of beg ch-4. *(12 dc, 12 ch-1 sps)*

Rnd 2: Ch 1, sc in same st as beg ch-1, ch 5, *sc in next st, ch 5, rep from * around, join in first sc. Fasten off. *(12 sc, 12 ch-5 sps)*

Rnd 3: Join B with dc in any ch-5 sp, ch 2, dc in same sp *(beg V-st made)*, ch 1, *(**V-st**—see Special Stitch, ch 1) in each rem ch-5 sp around, join in first dc. *(12 V-sts, 12 ch-1 sps)*

Rnd 4: **Ch 5** (see Pattern Notes), [dc in next st, ch 2] around, join in 3rd ch of beg ch-5. Fasten off. (24 dc, 24 ch-2 sps)

Rnd 5: Join A with sc in ch-2 sp above any V-st on rnd 3, ch 3, sc in same sp, *[sc in next st, 2 sc in next ch-2 sp] 3 times, sc in next st, (sc, ch 3, sc) in next ch-2 sp, rep from * 4 times, [sc in next st, 2 sc in next ch-2 sp] 3 times, sc in next st, join in first sc. Fasten off. (72 sc, 6 ch-3 sps)

HALF MOTIF
Row 1 (RS): With A, ch 5, **join** (see Pattern Notes) in first ch to form ring, **ch 4** (see Pattern Notes), [dc in ring, ch 1] 6 times, dc in ring, turn. (8 dc, 7 ch-1 sps)

Row 2: Ch 1, sc in first st, [ch 5, sc in next st] 7 times. Fasten off. (8 sc, 7 ch-5 sps)

Row 3: With RS facing, join B with dc in first ch-5 sp, ch 2, dc in same sp (beg V-st), ch 1, (V-st—see Special Stitch, ch 1) in each of next 5 ch-5 sps, V-st in last ch-5 sp, turn. (7 V-sts, 6 ch-1 sps)

Row 4: **Ch 5** (see Pattern Notes), [dc in next st, ch 2] 12 times, dc in last st. Fasten off. (14 dc, 13 ch-2 sps)

Row 5: With RS facing, join A with sc in first ch-2 sp, ch 3, sc in same sp, *[sc in next st, 2 sc in next ch-2 sp] 3 times, sc in next st**, (sc, ch 3, sc) in next ch-2 sp, rep from * twice, ending last rep at **, (sc, ch 3, sc) in last ch sp. Fasten off. (38 sc, 4 ch-3 sps) ∎

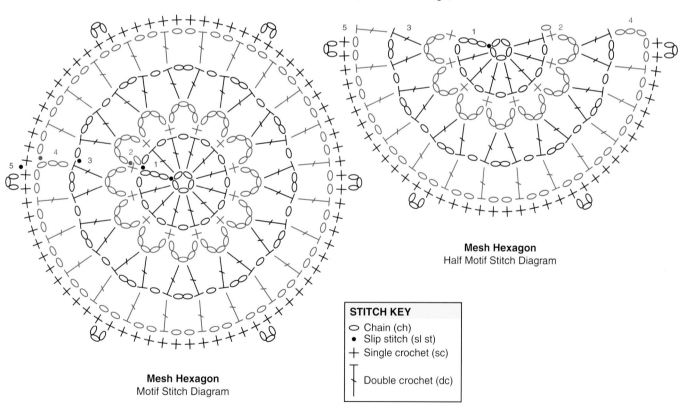

Mesh Hexagon
Motif Stitch Diagram

Mesh Hexagon
Half Motif Stitch Diagram

STITCH KEY
◦ Chain (ch)
• Slip stitch (sl st)
+ Single crochet (sc)
┬ Double crochet (dc)

Cardi Square

SKILL LEVEL

EASY

FINISHED MEASUREMENTS

Motif: 4½ inches x 4½ inches (side to side)

Half Motif: 6 inches x 3½ inches

MATERIALS

- Plymouth Encore Worsted medium (worsted) weight acrylic/wool yarn (3½ oz/200 yds/100g per ball):
  3 yds #355 garnet mix (A)
  2 yds #473 aquarius (B)
- Size I/9/5.5mm crochet hook or size needed to obtain gauge
- Tapestry needle

4 MEDIUM

GAUGE

Motif = 4½ inches x 4½ inches (blocked)

Take time to check gauge.

PATTERN NOTES

Weave in ends as work progresses.

Join with slip stitch as indicated unless otherwise stated.

Chain-3 at beginning of round or row counts as a double crochet unless otherwise stated.

MOTIF

Rnd 1 (RS): With A, ch 5, **join** (see Pattern Notes) in first ch to form ring, ch 1, [sc in ring, ch 3, sc in ring] 4 times, join in first sc. (8 sc, 4 ch-3 sps)

Rnd 2: Sl st in next ch-3 sp, **ch 3** (see Pattern Notes), 4 dc in same sp as beg ch-3, ch 1, *5 dc in next ch-3 sp, ch 1, rep from * twice, join in 3rd ch of beg ch-3. Fasten off. (20 dc, 4 ch-1 sps)

Rnd 3: Join B with dc in any ch-1 sp, *ch 1, 7 tr in 3rd dc of next 5-dc group, ch 1**, dc in next ch-1 sp, rep from * around, ending last rep at **, join in first dc. Fasten off. (28 tr, 4 dc, 8 ch-1 sps)

Rnd 4: Join A with sc in 4th tr of any 7-tr group, ch 5, sc in same st, ch 5, sc in next dc, ch 5, *(sc, ch 5, sc) in 4th tr of next 7-tr group, ch 5, sc in next dc, ch 5, rep from * around, join in first sc. (12 sc, 12 ch-5 sps)

HALF MOTIF

Row 1 (RS): With A, ch 5, **join** (see Pattern Notes) in first ch to form ring, ch 1, sc in ring, ch 3, [2 sc in ring, ch 3] twice, sc in ring, turn. (6 sc, 3 ch-3 sps)

Row 2: Ch 1, sl st in next ch-3 sp, **ch 3** (see Pattern Notes), 2 dc in same sp, ch 1, 5 dc in next ch-3 sp, ch 1, 3 dc in next ch-3 sp. Fasten off. (11 dc, 2 ch-1 sps)

Row 3: With RS facing, join B with tr in first st, 3 tr in same st, ch 1, dc in next ch-1 sp, ch 1, 7 tr in 3rd dc of next 5-dc group, ch 1, dc in next ch-1 sp, ch 1, 4 tr in last dc. Fasten off. (15 tr, 2 dc, 4 ch-1 sps)

Row 4: With WS facing, join A with sc in first st, ch 5, sc in same st, ch 5, sc in next dc, ch 5, (sc, ch 5, sc) in 4th tr of next 7-tr group, ch 5, sc in next dc, ch 5, (sc, ch 5, sc) in last st. Fasten off. ∎

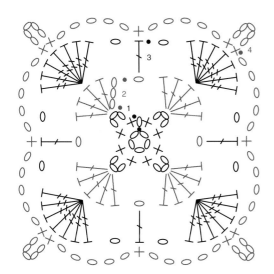

Cardi Square
Motif Stitch Diagram

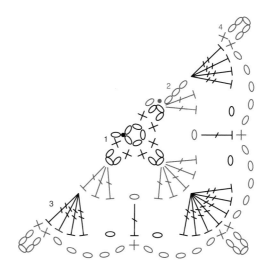

Cardi Square
Half Motif Stitch Diagram

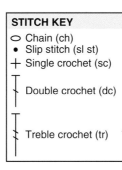

STITCH KEY
○ Chain (ch)
● Slip stitch (sl st)
+ Single crochet (sc)
Double crochet (dc)
Treble crochet (tr)

Pinky Perfect Hexagon

SKILL LEVEL

BEGINNER

FINISHED MEASUREMENTS

Motif: 6 inches x 6 inches (side to side)

Half Motif: 6½ inches wide x 3 inches tall

MATERIALS

- Plymouth Encore Worsted medium (worsted) weight acrylic/wool yarn (3½ oz/200 yds/100g per ball):
  4 yds each #1385 bright fuchsia (A) and #959 mauvetone (B)
- Size J/10/6mm crochet hook or size needed to obtain gauge
- Tapestry needle

GAUGE

Motif = 6 inches x 6 inches (blocked)

Take time to check gauge.

PATTERN NOTES

Weave in ends as work progresses.

Join with slip stitch as indicated unless otherwise stated.

Chain-3 at beginning of round or row counts as a double crochet unless otherwise stated.

MOTIF

Rnd 1 (RS): With A, ch 4, **join** (see Pattern Notes) in first ch to form ring, ch 1, 12 sc in ring, join in first sc. Fasten off. (12 sc)

Rnd 2: Join B with tr in any sc, tr in same st, 2 tr in each rem sc around, join in first tr. (24 tr)

Rnd 3: Ch 3 (see Pattern Notes), dc in same st as beg ch-3, 2 dc in each rem tr around, join in 3rd ch of beg ch-3. Fasten off. (48 dc)

Rnd 4: Join A with dc in any dc, dc in each of next 7 sts, ch 3, *dc in each of next 8 sts, ch 3, rep from * around, join in first dc. (48 dc, 6 ch-3 sps)

Rnd 5: Ch 1, sc in same st as beg ch-1, sc in each of next 7 sts, 3 sc in next ch-3 sp, [sc in each of next 8 sts, 3 sc in next ch-3 sp] 5 times, join in first sc. Fasten off.

HALF MOTIF

Row 1 (RS): With A, ch 4, **join** (see Pattern Notes) in first ch to form ring, ch 1, 7 sc in ring. Fasten off. (7 sc)

Row 2: With WS facing, join B with tr in first st, tr in same st, 2 tr in each rem st across, turn. (14 tr)

Row 3: Ch 3 (see Pattern Notes), 2 dc in each of next 12 sts, dc in last st. Fasten off. (26 dc)

Row 4: With WS facing, join A with dc in first st, ch 3, dc in each of next 8 sts, ch 3, rep from * twice, dc in last st, turn. (26 dc, 4 ch-3 sps)

Row 5: Ch 1, sk first st, 2 sc in next ch-3 sp, sc in each of next 8 sts, [3 sc in next ch-3 sp, sc in each of next 8 sts] twice, 2 sc in last ch-3 sp. Fasten off. (34 sc) ■

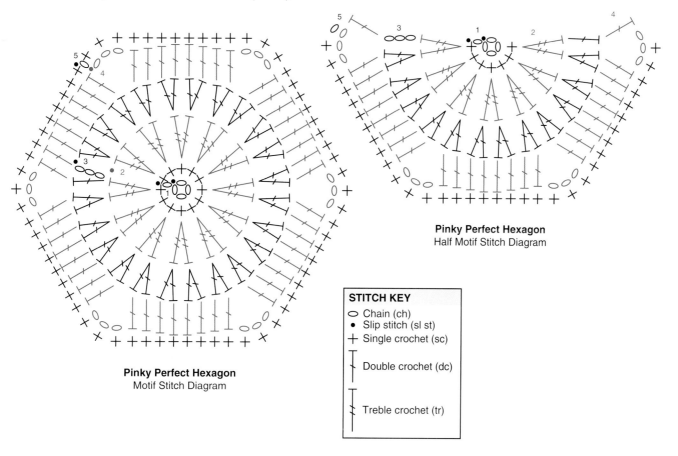

Pinky Perfect Hexagon
Motif Stitch Diagram

Pinky Perfect Hexagon
Half Motif Stitch Diagram

STITCH KEY
○ Chain (ch)
● Slip stitch (sl st)
+ Single crochet (sc)
┃ Double crochet (dc)
⌇ Treble crochet (tr)

Boysenberry Blanket

SKILL LEVEL

EASY

FINISHED MEASUREMENTS
54 inches wide x 64 inches long

MATERIALS
- Plymouth Encore Worsted medium (worsted) weight acrylic/wool yarn (3½ oz/200 yds/100g per ball):
  6 balls each #458 purple orchid (A) and #355 garnet mix (B)
  2 balls each #1385 bright fuchsia (C), #449 pink (D) and #514 light wedgewood (E)
- Size I/9/5.5mm crochet hook or size needed to obtain gauge
- Tapestry needle

GAUGE
Rnds 1–7 = 5½ inches

Take time to check gauge.

PATTERN NOTES
Weave in ends as work progresses.

Join with slip stitch as indicated unless otherwise stated.

Chain-3 at beginning of round counts as a double crochet unless otherwise stated.

SPECIAL STITCHES
Beginning cluster (beg cl): Ch 3, holding back last lp of each st on hook, 2 dc in same place as beg ch-3, yo and draw through 3 lps on hook.

Cluster (cl): Holding back last lp of each st on hook, 3 dc as indicated in instructions, yo and draw through 4 lps on hook.

BLANKET
MOTIF
Make 99.

Rnd 1 (RS): With C, ch 5, **join** (see Pattern Notes) in first ch to form ring, **ch 3** (see Pattern Notes), 15 dc in ring, join in 3rd ch of beg ch-3. Fasten off. (16 dc)

Rnd 2: Working in **back lps** (see Stitch Guide), join D with sc in any dc, sc in same st, 2 sc in each rem st around, join in first sc. Fasten off. (32 sc)

Rnd 3: Working through both lps, join A in same sc as joining, **beg cl** (see Special Stitches) in same st, ch 2, sk next st, *cl (see Special Stitches), ch 2, sk next st, rep from * 14 times, join in top of beg cl. (16 cls, 16 ch-2 sps)

Rnd 4: Ch 1, sc in same st as beg ch-1, 2 sc in next ch-2 sp, *sc in next cl, 2 sc in next ch-2 sp, rep from * around, join in first sc. Fasten off. (48 sc)

Rnd 5: Working in back lps, join E with sc in same sc as joining, sc in each rem st around, join in first sc. Fasten off.

Rnd 6: Working in back lps, join E with sc in same sc as joining, sc in same sc, sc in each of next 5 sts, *2 sc in next st, sc in each of next 5 sts, rep from * 6 times, join in first sc. (56 sc)

Rnd 7: Working through both lps, ch 3, dc in same st, ch 3 (corner sp made), 2 dc in next st, hdc in next st, sc in each of next 10 sts, [hdc in next st, 2 dc in next st, ch 3 (corner sp made), 2 dc in next st, hdc in next st, sc in each of next 10 sts] twice, hdc in next st, join in 3rd ch of beg ch-3. Fasten off. (40 sc, 8 hdc, 16 dc, 4 ch-3 corner sps)

ASSEMBLY

Arrange Motifs in 11 rows of 9 Motifs each. With RS facing and with tapestry needle, **whipstitch** (*see illustration*) Motifs tog through outer lps only.

Whipstitch

EDGING

Rnd 1 (RS): With RS facing and 1 short end at top, join B with sc in right-hand ch-3 corner sp, 2 sc in same sp (*beg corner made*), *[sc in each st to next Motif joining, 2 sc in first join sp, 2 sc in next join sp] 8 times, sc in each st to next ch-3 corner sp, 3 sc in ch-3 corner sp (*corner made*), [sc in each st to next Motif joining, 2 sc in first join sp, 2 sc in next join sp] 10 times, sc in each st to next ch-3 corner sp**, 3 sc in ch-3 corner sp (*corner made*), rep from * once, ending rep at **, join in first sc. Fasten off.

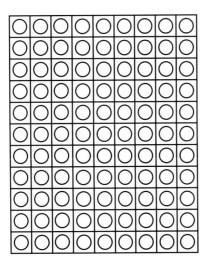

Boysenberry Blanket
Assembly Diagram

Rnd 2: Join C with sc in 2nd sc of any corner, 2 sc in same st, *sc in each st to 2nd sc of next corner**, 3 sc in 2nd sc of corner, rep from * around, ending last rep at **, join in first sc.

Rnd 3: [Ch 1, sl st in next st] around, join in joining sl st. Fasten off. ■

Blanket Square
Motif Stitch Diagram

STITCH KEY

○ Chain (ch)
⌒ Work in back loops
• Slip stitch (sl st)
+ Single crochet (sc)
T Half double crochet (hdc)
Ŧ Double crochet (dc)
⬭ Beginning cluster (beg cl)
⬭ Cluster (cl)

Scarf

SKILL LEVEL

INTERMEDIATE

FINISHED MEASUREMENTS
11 inches wide x 52 inches long

MATERIALS
- Plymouth Encore Worsted medium (worsted) weight acrylic/wool yarn (3½ oz/200 yds/100g per ball):
  2 balls #137 California pink (C)
  1 ball each #458 purple orchid (A) and #1308 beach berry (B)
- Size I/9/5.5mm crochet hook or size needed to obtain gauge
- Tapestry needle

GAUGE
Rnds 1–5 = 4¾ inches (blocked)

Take time to check gauge.

PATTERN NOTES
Weave in ends as work progresses.

Join with slip stitch as indicated unless otherwise stated.

Chain-4 at beginning of round or row counts as a treble crochet unless otherwise stated.

SPECIAL STITCHES
Beginning Bobble (beg bobble): Ch 1 loosely, *yo and draw up lp 4 times in st indicated, yo and draw through all lps on hook.

Bobble (bobble): *Yo and draw up lp 4 times in st indicated, yo and draw through all lps on hook.

SCARF
FIRST MOTIF
Rnd 1 (RS): With A, ch 4, **join** *(see Pattern Notes)* in first ch to form ring, ch 1, 6 sc in ring, join first sc. *(6 sc)*

Rnd 2: Beg bobble *(see Special Stitches)* in same st as joining, ch 3, [**bobble** *(see Special Stitches)*

in next st, ch 3] 5 times, join in top of beg bobble. Fasten off. *(6 bobbles, 6 ch-3 sps)*

Rnd 3: Join B with sc in top of any bobble, 3 sc in next ch-3 sp, [sc in top of next bobble, 3 sc in next ch-3 sp] 5 times, join in first sc. Fasten off. *(24 sc)*

Rnd 4: Join C in sc over any bobble, **ch 4** *(see Pattern Notes)*, 4 tr in same st, *ch 3, sk next 3 sts**, 5 tr in next st, rep from * around, ending last rep at **, join in 4th ch of beg ch-4. *(30 tr, 6 ch-3 sps)*

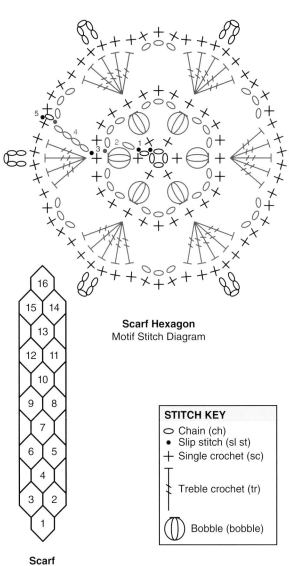

Scarf Hexagon
Motif Stitch Diagram

STITCH KEY
- ◯ Chain (ch)
- ● Slip stitch (sl st)
- ✛ Single crochet (sc)
- ⊤ Treble crochet (tr)
- ⬭ Bobble (bobble)

Scarf
Diagram

Rnd 5: Ch 1, sc in same ch as beg ch-1, sc in next st, *(sc, ch 5, sc) in next st, sc in each of next 2 sts, 3 sc in next ch-3 sp**, sc in each of next 2 sts, rep from * around, ending last rep at **, join in first sc. Fasten off. *(54 sc, 6 ch-5 sps)*

2ND MOTIF
Note: Refer to diagram for placement of following Motifs.

Rnds 1–4: Rep rnds 1–4 of First Motif.

Rnd 5: Ch 1, sc in same ch as beg ch-1, sc in next st, (sc, ch 2, sl st in ch-5 sp on adjacent Motif, ch 2, sc) in next st, sc in each of next 2 sts, 3 sc in next ch-3 sp, sc in each of next 2 sts, (sc, ch 2, sl st in next ch-5 sp on adjacent Motif, ch 2, sc) in next st, sc in each of next 2 sts, 3 sc in next ch-3 sp, sc in each of next 2 sts, *(sc, ch 5 sc) in next st, sc in next 2 sts, 3 sc in next ch-3 sp**, sc in each of next 2 sts, rep from *

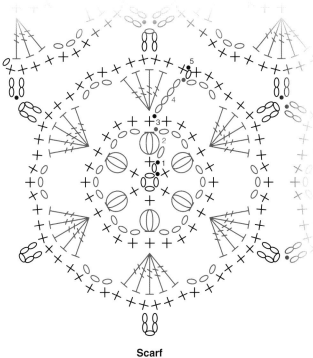

Scarf
Motif Joining Stitch Diagram

around, ending last rep at **, join in first sc. Fasten off. *(54 sc, 6 ch-5 sps)*

3RD–16TH MOTIFS

Work same as 2nd Motif, joining sides in similar manner.

HALF MOTIF
Make 8.

Note: Work Half Motifs referring to diagram for placement.

Row 1 RS): With C, ch 3, **join** *(see Pattern Notes)* in first ch to form ring, ch 1, 4 sc in ring, turn. *(4 sc)*

Row 2: Beg bobble *(see Special Stitches)* in first st, [ch 3, **bobble** *(see Special Stitches)* in next st] 3 times. Fasten off. *(4 bobbles, 3 ch-3 sps)*

Row 3: With RS facing, join B with sc in first bobble, [3 sc in next ch-3 sp, sc in next bobble] 3 times. Fasten off. *(13 sc)*

Row 4: With WS facing, join A in first st, **ch 4** *(see Pattern Notes)*, 2 tr in same st, [ch 3, sk next 3 sc, 5 tr in next sc] twice, ch 3, sk next 3 sc, 3 tr in last sc, turn. *(16 tr, 3 ch-3 sps)*

Row 5: Ch 1, (sc, ch 2, sl st in ch-5 sp on adjacent Motif, ch 2, sc) in first st, sc in each of next 2 sts, 3 sc in next ch-3 sp, sc in each of next 2 sts, *(sc, ch 2, sl st in next ch-5 joining, ch 2, sc) in next st, sc in each of next 2 sts, 3 sc in next ch-3 sp, sc in each of next 2 sts, rep from * once, (sc, ch 2, sl st in next ch-5 sp on adjacent Motif, ch 2, sc) in next st, sc in each of next 2 sts, 3 sc in next ch-3 sp, sc in each of next 2 sts. Fasten off.

EDGING
Rnd 1: Working around entire Scarf, work as follows:

A. With RS facing and 1 short end at top, join C with sc in top center ch-5 sp of Motif, 6 sc in same sp, ch 2, sk next 3 sts, sc in each of next 3 sts, ch 2, sk next 3 sts, 7 sc in next ch-5 sp, ch 2, sk next 3 sts, sc in each of next 3 sts, ch 2, sk next 3 sts, 2 sc in next joined sp;

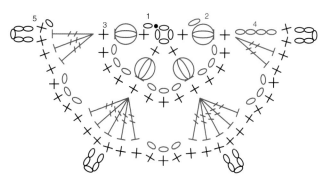

Scarf Hexagon
Half Motif Stitch Diagram

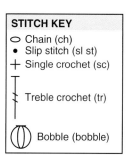

STITCH KEY
◯ Chain (ch)
• Slip stitch (sl st)
+ Single crochet (sc)
⊤ Treble crochet (tr)
⬯ Bobble (bobble)

B. working on next Motif, 2 sc in next joined sp, ch 2, sk next 3 sts, sc in each of next 3 sts, ch 2, sk next 3 sts, 7 sc in next ch-5 sp, ch 2, sk next 3 sts, sc in each of next 3 sts, ch 2, sk next 3 sts, 2 sc in next joined sp;

C. *working on next Half Motif, 2 sc in next joined sp, 3 sc in side of next st, sc in side of next sc row, sc in gap between sc row and next cl, ch 2, sc in beg ch-4 ring, ch 2, sc in gap between next cl and next sc row, sc in side of sc row, 3 sc in side of next st, 2 sc in next joined sp;

D. working on next Motif, 2 sc in next joined sp, ch 2, sk next 3 sts, sc in each of next 3 sts, ch 2, sk next 3 sts, 2 sc in next joined sp*;

E. rep from * to * twice;

F. rep step C;

G. rep step B;

H. 2 sc in joined sp, ch 2, sk next 3 sts, sc in each of next 3 sts, ch 2, sk next 3 sts, [7 sc in next ch-5 sp, ch 2, sk next 3 sts, sc in each of next 3 sts, ch 2, sk next 3 sts] twice, sc in each of next 3 sts, ch 2, sk next 3 sts, 2 sc in next joined sp;

I. rep step B;

J. rep from * to * 3 times;

K. rep step C;

L. rep step B;

M. 2 sc in next joined sp, ch 2, sk next 3 sts, sc in each of next 3 sts, ch 2, sk next 3 sts, 7 sc in next ch-5 sp, ch 2, sk next 3 sts, sc in each of next 3 sts, ch 2, sk next 3 sts, join in first sc.

Rnd 2: Ch 1, sc in each st and ch around, join in first sc. Fasten off. ∎

Hat

SKILL LEVEL

EASY

FINISHED MEASUREMENT
16 inches (unstretched to fit 22-inch head)

MATERIALS

- Plymouth Encore Worsted medium (worsted) weight acrylic/wool yarn (3½ oz/200 yds/100g per ball): 1 ball #1385 bright fuchsia
- Size I/9/5.5mm crochet hook or size needed to obtain gauge
- Tapestry needle

GAUGE
Rnds 1 –6 = 6 inches (blocked); 14 sc = 4 inches

Take time to check gauge.

PATTERN NOTES
Join with slip stitch as indicated unless otherwise stated.

Chain-3 at beginning of round counts as a double crochet unless otherwise stated.

Chain-2 at beginning of round counts as a half double crochet unless otherwise stated.

HAT
Rnd 1 (RS): Ch 4, **join** (see Pattern Notes) in first ch to form ring, **ch 3** (see Pattern Notes), 11 dc in ring, join in 3rd ch of beg ch-3. (12 dc)

Rnd 2: Ch 1, sc in same st as beg ch-1, ch 9, sc in same st, (sc, ch 5, sc) in next st, *(sc, ch 9, sc) in next st, (sc, ch 5, sc) in next st, rep from * 4 times, join in first sc. (6 ch-9 sps, 6 ch-5 sps)

Rnd 3: Sl st in each of next 4 chs of next ch-9 sp, ch 1, 3 sc in same sp, *ch 2, sc in next ch-5 sp, ch 2**, 3 sc in next ch-9 sp, rep from * around, ending last rep at **, join in first sc. (24 sc, 12 ch-2 sps)

Rnd 4: Ch 1, sc in same st as beg ch-1, *(sc, ch 5, sc) in next sc, sc in next sc, 2 sc in next ch-2 sp, sc in next sc, 2 sc in next ch-2 sp**, sc in next sc, rep from * around, ending last rep at **, join in first sc. (54 sc, 6 ch-5 sps)

Rnd 5: Sl st in next sc and in each of next 2 chs of next ch-5 sp, 3 sc in same ch-5 sp, ch 3, sk next 4 sts, sc in next st, ch 3, sk next 4 sts, *3 sc in next ch-5 sp, ch 3, sk next 4 sts, sc in next st, ch 3, sk next 4 sts, rep from * 4 times, join in first sc. (24 sc, 12 ch-3 sps)

Rnd 6: Ch 1, sc in same st as beg ch-1, sc in each of next 2 sc, *3 sc in next ch-3 sp, sc in next sc, 3 sc in next ch-3 sp**, sc in each of next 3 sc, rep from * around, ending last rep at **, join in first sc. (60 sc)

Rnd 7: Ch 1, sc in same st as beg ch-1, ch 5, sk next 2 sc, *sc in next sc, ch 5, sk next 2 sc, rep from * around, join in first sc. *(20 sc, 20 ch-5 sps)*

Rnd 8: Ch 1, sc in same st as beg ch-1, 3 sc in next ch-5 sp, *sc in next sc, 3 sc in next ch-5 sp, rep from * around, join in first sc. *(80 sc)*

Rnd 9: Ch 1, sc in each sc around, join in first sc.

Rnd 10: Ch 3, dc in each rem st around, join in 3rd ch of beg ch-3.

Rnds 11–13: Rep rnd 10.

Rnd 14: Ch 2 *(see Pattern Notes)*, **fpdc** *(see Stitch Guide)* around post of next st, sk next st, *fpdc around post of each of next 2 sts, sk next st, fpdc around post of next st, sk

next st, rep from * to last st, fpdc around post of last st, join in 2nd ch of beg ch-2. *(47 fpdc, 1 hdc)*

Rnds 15–18: Ch 2, fpdc around each fpdc around, join in 2nd ch of beg ch-2. At end of last rnd, fasten off. ■

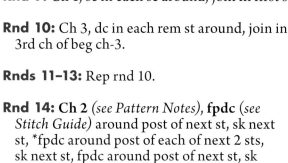

STITCH KEY
- ◯ Chain (ch)
- • Slip stitch (sl st)
- ✛ Single crochet (sc)
- ↟ Double crochet (dc)
- ↟ Front post double crochet (fpdc)

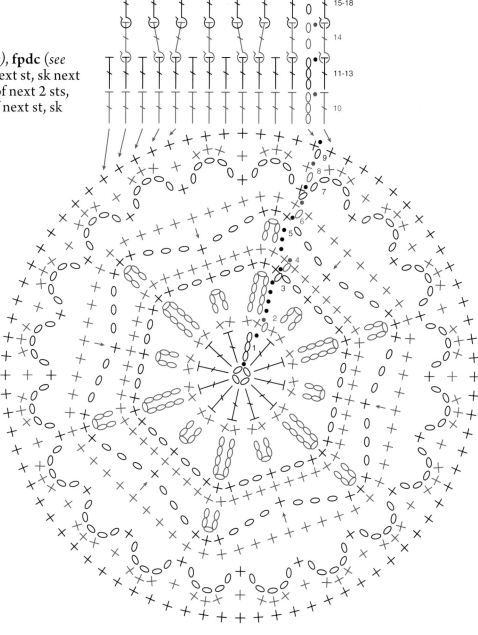

Hat
Stitch Diagram

Cowl

SKILL LEVEL
■■■□
INTERMEDIATE

FINISHED MEASUREMENTS
25½ inches x 11 inches (when joined and laid flat)

MATERIALS
- Plymouth Encore Worsted medium (worsted) weight acrylic/wool yarn (3½ oz/200 yds/100g per ball):
  2 balls #355 garnet mix
  1 ball #453 rust roadster
- Size J/10/6mm crochet hook or size needed to obtain gauge
- Tapestry needle

GAUGE
Rnds 1–4 = 4 inches (blocked)

Take time to check gauge.

PATTERN NOTES
Weave in ends as work progresses.

Join with slip stitch as indicated unless otherwise stated.

Chain-3 at beginning of round counts as a double crochet unless otherwise stated.

SPECIAL STITCHES
Cluster (cl): Holding back last lp of each st on hook, 3 dc as indicated in instructions, yo and draw through 4 lps on hook.

Beginning cluster (beg cl): Ch 3, holding back last lp of each st on hook, 2 dc in same sp as beg ch-3, yo and draw through 3 lps on hook.

Picot: Ch 3, hdc in 3rd ch from hook.

COWL
MOTIF A
Rnd 1 (RS): With A, ch 5, **join** (see Pattern Notes) in first ch to form ring, **ch 3** (see Pattern Notes),

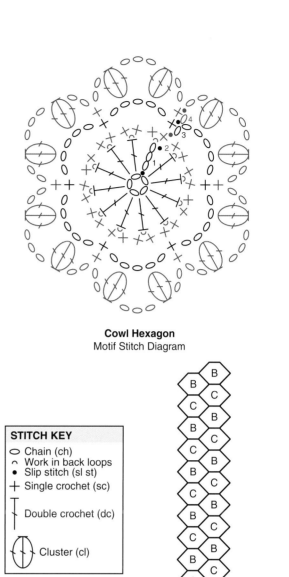

Cowl Hexagon
Motif Stitch Diagram

STITCH KEY
◯ Chain (ch)
⌒ Work in back loops
• Slip stitch (sl st)
+ Single crochet (sc)
∤ Double crochet (dc)
⬭ Cluster (cl)

Cowl
Diagram

11 dc in ring, join in 3rd ch of beg ch-3. Fasten off. *(12 dc)*

Rnd 2: Working in **back lps** *(see Stitch Guide)*, join B with sc in any st, sc in same st, 2 sc in each rem st around, join in first sc. *(24 sc)*

Rnd 3: Ch 1, sc in same st as beg ch-1, ch 5, sk next 3 sts, [sc in next st, ch 5, sk next 3 sts] 5 times, join in first sc. *(6 sc, 6 ch-5 sps)*

Rnd 4: Ch 1, sc in same sc as beg ch-1, *ch 2, (**cl**—see Special Stitches, ch 3, cl) in next ch-5 sp, ch 2**, sc in next st, rep from * around, ending last rep at **, join in first sc. Fasten off. *(12 cls, 6 sc, 12 ch-2 sps, 6 ch-3 sps)*

Note: Refer to diagram for placement of following Motifs.

MOTIF B
Rnd 1: With B, rep rnd 1 of Motif A.

Rnds 2 & 3: With A, rep rnds 2 and 3 of Motif A.

Rnd 4: Ch 1, sc in same sc, (ch 2, cl, ch 1, sl st in ch-3 sp on adjacent motif, ch 1) in next ch-5 sp, ch 2, sc in next st, ch 2, (ch 2, cl, ch 1, sl st in next ch-3 sp on adjacent motif, ch 1) in next ch-5 sp, ch 2, sc in next st,*ch 2, (cl, ch 3, cl) in next ch-5 sp, ch 2, sc in next st, ch 2**, sc in next st, rep from * around, ending last rep at **, join in first sc. Fasten off. *(12 cls, 6 sc, 12 ch-2 sps, 6 ch-3 sps)*

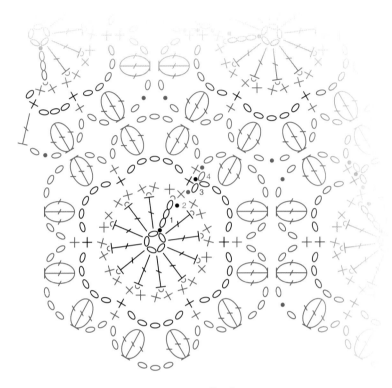

Cowl
Motif Joining Stitch Diagram

MOTIF C
With A, work same as Motif B, joining sides in similar manner.

Following diagram, rep Motifs B and C until 24 Motifs have been completed, joining last 2 Motifs to first 2 Motifs to form cowl.

EDGING
Rnd 1: With RS facing and working around long edge, join A in joined sp on Motif B *(see arrow on assembly diagram)*, **beg cl** *(see Special Stitches)* in same sp, *ch 2, sc in next sc, ch 2, (cl, ch 3, cl) in next ch-3 sp, ch 2, sc in next sc, ch 2, cl in next joined sp, ch 3, cl in joined sp on next Motif, rep from * 10 times, ch 2, sc in next sc, ch 2, (cl, ch 3, cl) in next ch-3 sp, ch 2, sc in next sc, ch 2, cl in next joined sp, join in top of beg cl.

Rnd 2: Ch 1, sc in same cl as beg ch-1, *2 sc in next ch-2 sp, sc in next sc, 2 sc in next ch-2 sp, sc in next cl, (2 sc, **picot**—*see Special Stitches*, 2 sc) in next ch-3 sp, sc in next cl, 2 sc in next ch-2 sp, sc in next sc, 2 sc in next ch-2 sp, sc in next cl, (2 sc, picot, 2 sc) in next ch-3 sp**, sc in next cl, rep from * around, ending last rep at **, join in first sc. Fasten off.

Rep rnds 1 and 2 on opposite long edge. ∎

STITCH GUIDE

STITCH ABBREVIATIONS

beg .... begin/begins/beginning
bpdc .... back post double crochet
bpsc ....back post single crochet
bptr ....back post treble crochet
CC .... contrasting color
ch(s) ....chain(s)
ch- .... refers to chain or space
previously made (i.e., ch-1 space)
ch sp(s) .... chain space(s)
cl(s) .... cluster(s)
cm .... centimeter(s)
dc .... double crochet (singular/plural)
dc dec .... double crochet 2 or more
stitches together, as indicated
dec .... decrease/decreases/decreasing
dtr .... double treble crochet
ext ....extended
fpdc .... front post double crochet
fpsc .... front post single crochet
fptr .... front post treble crochet
g ....gram(s)
hdc .... half double crochet
hdc dec .... half double crochet 2 or more
stitches together, as indicated
inc .... increase/increases/increasing
lp(s) ....loop(s)
MC ....main color
mm .... millimeter(s)
oz ....ounce(s)
pc .... popcorn(s)
rem .... remain/remains/remaining
rep(s) ....repeat(s)
rnd(s) .... round(s)
RS .... right side
sc .... single crochet (singular/plural)
sc dec ....single crochet 2 or more
stitches together, as indicated
sk ....skip/skipped/skipping
sl st(s) .... slip stitch(es)
sp(s) .... space(s)/spaced
st(s) .... stitch(es)
tog ....together
tr .... treble crochet
trtr ....triple treble
WS .... wrong side
yd(s) ....yard(s)
yo .... yarn over

YARN CONVERSION

OUNCES TO GRAMS		GRAMS TO OUNCES	
1	28.4	25	⅞
2	56.7	40	1⅔
3	85.0	50	1¾
4	113.4	100	3½

UNITED STATES		UNITED KINGDOM
sl st (slip stitch)	=	sc (single crochet)
sc (single crochet)	=	dc (double crochet)
hdc (half double crochet)	=	htr (half treble crochet)
dc (double crochet)	=	tr (treble crochet)
tr (treble crochet)	=	dtr (double treble crochet)
dtr (double treble crochet)	=	ttr (triple treble crochet)
skip	=	miss

Reverse single crochet (reverse sc): Ch 1, sk first st, working from left to right, insert hook in next st from front to back, draw up lp on hook, yo and draw through both lps on hook.

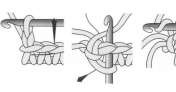

Chain (ch): Yo, pull through lp on hook.

Single crochet (sc): Insert hook in st, yo, pull through st, yo, pull through both lps on hook.

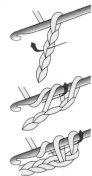

Double crochet (dc): Yo, insert hook in st, yo, pull through st, [yo, pull through 2 lps] twice.

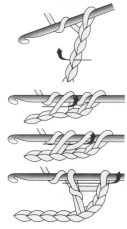

Front loop (front lp) Back loop (back lp)

Front Loop   Back Loop

Front post stitch (fp): Back post stitch (bp): When working post st, insert hook from right to left around post of st on previous row.

Back   Front

Post of Stitch

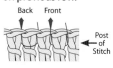

Half double crochet (hdc): Yo, insert hook in st, yo, pull through st, yo, pull through all 3 lps on hook.

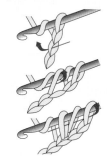

Double treble crochet (dtr): Yo 3 times, insert hook in st, yo, pull through st, [yo, pull through 2 lps] 4 times.

Slip stitch (sl st): Insert hook in st, pull through both lps on hook.

Chain color change (ch color change) Yo with new color, draw through last lp on hook.

Double crochet color change (dc color change) Drop first color, yo with new color, draw through last 2 lps of st.

Treble crochet (tr): Yo twice, insert hook in st, yo, pull through st, [yo, pull through 2 lps] 3 times.

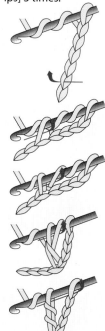

Single crochet decrease (sc dec): (Insert hook, yo, draw lp through) in each of the sts indicated, yo, draw through all lps on hook.

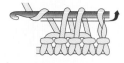

Example of 2-sc dec

Half double crochet decrease (hdc dec): (Yo, insert hook, yo, draw lp through) in each of the sts indicated, yo, draw through all lps on hook.

Example of 2-hdc dec

Double crochet decrease (dc dec): (Yo, insert hook, yo, draw lp through, yo, draw through 2 lps on hook) in each of the sts indicated, yo, draw through all lps on hook.

Example of 2-dc dec

Treble crochet decrease (tr dec): Holding back last lp of each st, tr in each of the sts indicated, yo, pull through all lps on hook.

Example of 2-tr dec

Metric Conversion Charts

METRIC CONVERSIONS

yards	x	.9144	=	metres (m)
yards	x	91.44	=	centimetres (cm)
inches	x	2.54	=	centimetres (cm)
inches	x	25.40	=	millimetres (mm)
inches	x	.0254	=	metres (m)

centimetres	x	.3937	=	inches
metres	x	1.0936	=	yards

INCHES INTO MILLIMETRES & CENTIMETRES (Rounded off slightly)

inches	mm	cm	inches	cm	inches	cm	inches	cm
1/8	3	0.3	5	12.5	21	53.5	38	96.5
1/4	6	0.6	5 1/2	14	22	56	39	99
3/8	10	1	6	15	23	58.5	40	101.5
1/2	13	1.3	7	18	24	61	41	104
5/8	15	1.5	8	20.5	25	63.5	42	106.5
3/4	20	2	9	23	26	66	43	109
7/8	22	2.2	10	25.5	27	68.5	44	112
1	25	2.5	11	28	28	71	45	114.5
1 1/4	32	3.2	12	30.5	29	73.5	46	117
1 1/2	38	3.8	13	33	30	76	47	119.5
1 3/4	45	4.5	14	35.5	31	79	48	122
2	50	5	15	38	32	81.5	49	124.5
2 1/2	65	6.5	16	40.5	33	84	50	127
3	75	7.5	17	43	34	86.5		
3 1/2	90	9	18	46	35	89		
4	100	10	19	48.5	36	91.5		
4 1/2	115	11.5	20	51	37	94		

KNITTING NEEDLES CONVERSION CHART

Canada/U.S.	0	1	2	3	4	5	6	7	8	9	10	10½	11	13	15
Metric (mm)	2	2¼	2¾	3¼	3½	3¾	4	4½	5	5½	6	6½	8	9	10

CROCHET HOOKS CONVERSION CHART

Canada/U.S.	1/B	2/C	3/D	4/E	5/F	6/G	8/H	9/I	10/J	10½/K	N
Metric (mm)	2.25	2.75	3.25	3.5	3.75	4.25	5	5.5	6	6.5	9.0

Annie's ® *Marvelous Crochet Motifs* is published by Annie's, 306 East Parr Road, Berne, IN 46711. Printed in USA. Copyright © 2014 Annie's. All rights reserved. This publication may not be reproduced in part or in whole without written permission from the publisher.

RETAIL STORES: If you would like to carry this pattern book or any other Annie's publication, visit AnniesWSL.com.

Every effort has been made to ensure that the instructions in this pattern book are complete and accurate. We cannot, however, take responsibility for human error, typographical mistakes or variations in individual work. Please visit AnniesCustomerCare.com to check for pattern updates.

ISBN: 978-1-57367-473-7

1 2 3 4 5 6 7 8 9